Hour of Consummation
(God's Prophetic Calendar of Time)

by E. Richard Bridgeforth, Sr.

PublishAmerica
Baltimore

First printing

At the specific preference of the author, PublishAmerica allowed this work to remain exactly as the author intended, verbatim, without editorial input.

Unless otherwise indicated, Bible quotations are taken from the King James Version (Scoffield Edition) of the Bible. Copyright © 2006 By World Prophetic Outreach Ministries.

ISBN: 1-4241-3529-X
PUBLISHED BY PUBLISHAMERICA, LLLP
www.publishamerica.com
Baltimore

Printed in the United States of America

Acknowledgements

I would like to acknowledge those who have contributed their time and efforts in the writing of this book. Without their help, I would have had a very hard time in getting this material published. I wish to express my sincere thanks to each of the following persons for their contributions.

Katherine V. Bridgeforth—My wife

My wife has spent many hours in proofreading and critiquing the material in this book. Furthermore, she has been continually supportive and has offered much encouragement. During the writing of this material, she has often helped me with sentence structuring, proper use of punctuation and material outlines. For her time invested in doing all of this, I express my most sincere gratitude.

Pastor Ronny Davis—Pastor of Living Water Fellowship, Bellingham, WA

Pastor Ronny Davis and his wife, Lori, are the Pastor's of Living Water Fellowship in Bellingham, WA. I wish to express my thanks to them for their continued encouragement, prayers and support. Furthermore, I wish to express my most sincere appreciation for the amount of time and effort that Pastor Ronny contributed in proofreading and critiquing the material in this book. Also, I want to thank him for taking time out of his very busy schedule to write the Foreword for this book.

Carl Frombly—Board Member and friend at Living Water Fellowship, Bellingham, WA

I wish to express my sincere appreciation to Carl Frombly for his contribution to this book. He is very active at Living

Water Fellowship, where he runs the soundboard, leads a small group fellowship and serves on the church board. He loves to study and search for answers to the questions posed by his small group attendees using as many resources as are available to him. Carl was very inspiring in suggesting the title to this book.

CONTENTS

Foreword

If there's one phrase you hear over and over in reference to the book of Revelation it is the phrase "hard to understand." The writing of John's vision itself is a supernatural phenomenon. The mere fact it is God's revelation to man tells us that the events foretold are things that mankind could not have *"sifted out by the reasonings of human understanding"* as Matthew Henry so aptly stated. Also, John wrote of things the earth had never dreamed of in his day but he could only write in the language of 100 A.D.

I'm convinced that much of what John saw and wrote about was somewhat confusing to him at the time. Regardless, as the Holy Spirit provided inspiration, John was faithful to write what was revealed to him so that we could catch a glimpse of future events. Because of the fact that the contents of the Revelation are the deep things of God being revealed to man by the Holy Spirit and the limitations placed on John by his humanity, the reading of the book of Revelation is, many times, placed on the back burner of our reading agenda.

Yet, as I read this book by E. Richard Bridgeforth, Sr., the book of Revelation is presented and explained in words that are simple but brimming with clarity. This book is probably not for the student of Revelation looking for a "new" slant on Scripture. However, if you are the average person who sincerely desires to understand John's writings of Revelation, you are in for a pleasant experience. Whether you are a new believer or a seasoned follower of Jesus who has somewhat guiltily avoided the book of Revelation, you will be blessed by reading this book.

Take your time, settle into your favorite reading spot, and enjoy! Let me warn you; don't be surprised if you have a hard time putting it down before you finish.

Ronny D. Davis
Pastor—Living Water Fellowship

Introduction

Many people feel nervous and sometimes fearful when they hear the end-time message preached. Some do not understand Revelation; therefore, they tend to shy away from reading the book. But the message of the last days is not a fearful message. It is not a message of doom and gloom as some think. For the child of God, it should be exciting and a joy to read! Most events found in Revelation do not affect today's Christians provided they are truly born again. A truly born again believer today will not be on the earth during the time the events of Revelation take place. They will have been *"caught up"* (1 Thess. 4:17) to be with Jesus! Jesus has given many promises to His followers pertaining to keeping them from the trials of the Tribulation period. One such promise is found in Revelation 3:10 where we are told, *"Because you have guarded and kept My word of patient endurance—have held fast the lesson of My patience with the expectant endurance that I give you— I also will keep you (safe) from the hour of trial (testing) which is coming on the whole world, to try those who dwell upon the earth."* (Amplified Version) Those that should experience fear when hearing the last day message are those that are not ready for Jesus' return and the sinners. Those who are not ready to meet the Lord at the time of the Rapture of the Church will have to remain on the earth to endure the trials that will come upon the entire world during the time after the Church is *"caught up."*

If ever there was a time to be more aware of the soon return of Jesus, it is now! We are living in the closing hours of the Church Age. Soon Jesus will be coming to gather His Church and take them to a place of *"many mansions."* (St. John 14:2) Jesus told us to *"Watch, therefore; for ye know not what hour your Lord doth come."* (St. Matt. 24:42) God's people need to be prepared for His soon return! They need to get busy and help others to get ready and be watching for the coming of the *"KING OF KINGS, AND LORD OF LORDS."* (Rev. 19:16)

There have been many books written concerning the last day message. In writing this book, I do not pretend to think that I can do a better work than someone else. My purpose of writing this book is to make it as simple as possible so that the average child of God can understand what the last day message is saying. I have read many books by many great authors who have written about the Book of Revelation. However, many of them are very hard to understand. The authors, although they are trying to explain the meaning of many things, tend to use words that are beyond the understanding of many Christians. They use Greek and Hebrew words, and they explain those words excellently. But to the average Christian, it is hard to keep on track when authors use what I like to call "high-dollar" words in writing about a certain topic. Therefore, I wanted to write about this great end-time message and put it in every day language to make it more understandable for the average person.

Furthermore, I have felt led of God to write this book for many years. I have studied the Bible and have done much research. (As stated above, I have read many books written by many authors concerning the end-time message. If at any time within this book it seems that I may have written something that is similar to what others have written, it is innocently and wholly coincidental. It is *NOT* my intention to copy any work done by others. After all, I have studied and researched the *BEST* material available.) I prayed for guidance and I have asked God for His help in writing this book. The desire to write became so overwhelming that I had to try. My only desire in writing this book is to make it simple to understand and to perhaps help others to come to a greater knowledge of God's Word. Also, I desire that others will come to know Jesus as their personal Savior. If you are not a born again child of God and if by reading this book you have decided to allow Jesus into your heart as your Lord and Savior, then I will have achieved my goal.

It is my sincere prayer that you will enjoy reading this book, and that it will be a blessing to you. In writing this, I have followed the leading of the Spirit and have written what I believe will help many to understand the message of the last days. May the Holy Spirit impress His presence upon you as you read this book!

Chapter One
THE PROPHECY OF THE SEVENTY WEEKS

"Seventy weeks (of years, or four hundred and ninety years) are decreed upon your people and upon your holy city Jerusalem, to finish and put an end to transgression, to seal up and make full the measure of sin, to purge away and make expiation and reconciliation for sin, and to bring in everlasting righteousness (permanent spiritual and moral rectitude in every area and relation) and to seal up vision and prophecy and prophet, and to anoint a holy of holies." (Dan. 9:24 Amplified Bible)

To understand this prophecy, we must realize that Daniel was concerned about the period of time that Israel would be persecuted. In Dan. 9:2 (Amp.) we find that he *"understood from the books the number of years, which according to the word of the Lord to Jeremiah the prophet must pass by before the desolations which had been pronounced on Jerusalem should end, and it was seventy years."* Daniel then spent much time in prayer and fasting (vs. 3 Amp.). He confessed the sins of Israel (vss. 4-15 Amp.) and asked God to forgive the people of Israel (vs. 19 Amp.). It was while he was praying when the angel, Gabriel, *"came near to me and touched me about the time of the evening sacrifice."* (vs. 21 Amp.) It was at this time when this prophecy was given to Daniel.

The people of Israel had turned their hearts from God and had gotten into worshipping idols. Daniel said that they had

13

"sinned and dealt perversely and done wickedly and have rebelled, turning aside from Your commandments and ordinances." (Dan. 9:5 Amp.) The people of Israel had not *"listened to and heeded Your servants the prophets, who spoke in Your name to our kings, our princes, and our fathers, and to all the people of the land."* (vs. 6 Amp.) Because they failed to do as they should have done, Israel became the captives of Babylon, then the Medes and the Persians and finally ruled by the Romans.

As stated above, Daniel understood from reading the Book of Jeremiah that Israel must *"serve the kings of Babylon seventy years."* (Jer. 25:11 Amp.) Israel would be captive and held in slavery in Babylon for this seventy-year period of time. It was during the period of Israel's captivity when the prophecy of the *"Seventy weeks"* was spoken to Daniel by the angel, Gabriel.

Daniel was told by the angel that *"Seventy weeks (of years, or four hundred and ninety years) are decreed upon your people and upon your holy city Jerusalem…"* The *"Seventy weeks"* are a period of time that is prophesied to Daniel that would come upon the Jews and Jerusalem. How do we determine what this period of time represents? If we interpret the seventy weeks as seventy weeks of seven years, we would then find the answer. Seventy weeks of seven years represents a total of 490 years. But how do we come up with the *"weeks of years"* terminology? We have to dig into the Word to find this answer.

We must understand that the *"weeks of years"* are an important time measure in the Jewish calendar. Let's look at Lev. 25:1-22. Here, God speaks to Moses, and tells him to *"speak unto the children of Israel, and say unto them, When ye come into the land which I shall give you, then shall the land keep a sabbath unto the Lord. Six years shalt thou sow thy field, and six years shalt thou prune thy vineyard, and gather in the fruit thereof; But in the seventh year shall be a sabbath of rest unto the land, a sabbath for the Lord: thou shalt neither sow thy field nor prune thy vineyard."* (vss.

2-4) Then in the eighth verse we are told, *"And thou shalt number seven sabbaths of years unto thee, seven times seven years."* The people of Israel were instructed by God that they were to work the land for a period of six years, but in the seventh year they were not to work the land, for this seventh year was to be a sabbath, a time of rest. They are told they are to number seven sabbaths of years, seven times seven years, which comes to a total of 49 years. (Lev. 25:8) The fiftieth year then was to become a year of *"jubilee."* (vss. 9-17) Then in Lev. 26 we are told that Israel is warned that *"if ye will not hearken unto me, and will not do all these commandments;.... I also will do this unto you."* (vss. 14-16) Then from verse 16 through 39, there are chastisements given. As we now know, Israel did break covenant with God and as a result they were scattered throughout the nations of the world. (Lev.26:32-35) Israel was ruled by the Babylonian Empire and the Jews were enslaved for a period of *"seventy years."* (Jer. 25:11; See also Dan. 9:2) Therefore, in keeping with the practice of understanding a *"week"* to be seven years, Daniel is told that 490 years are determined upon his people and upon his holy city, Jerusalem. It must be understood that because Israel broke covenant with God and did not keep the sabbath years as instructed, and because they worshipped idols and did *"despise my statutes"* (Lev. 26:15), then God allowed them to be scattered and enslaved for a period of *"seventy years."* (Jer. 25:11) The prophecy of the Seventy weeks is a result of Israel's stubbornness toward God. Therefore, this period of time is set apart from all other time. It is a specific period of time that God will be dealing with Israel.

To further show how we come to the knowledge that a *"week"* in God's prophetic calendar of time is in reference to seven years, we need to look at the story of Jacob. In Gen. 28:2 we are told that Jacob was instructed to go to the house of *"Bethuel, thy mother's father; and take thee a wife from there of the daughters of Laban."* We know the story of how Jacob worked for Laban to earn Rachel, Laban's younger daughter, as his wife. He said, *"I will serve thee seven years for Rachel, thy younger daughter."* (Gen. 29:18) Laban agreed to this (vs.19) and Jacob *"served seven years for Rachel."* (vs.20) When he had finished the seven years, Jacob asked that he be given his wife, and we know how Laban gave his older daughter, Leah, to Jacob instead. (Gen.29:21-24) Jacob was not happy about this and questioned Laban as to why he had done this. (vs.25) Laban said, *"It must not be so done in our country, to give the younger before the first-born. Fulfill her week, and we will give thee this also for the service which thou shalt serve with me yet seven other years. And Jacob did so, and fulfilled her week; and he gave him Rachel, his daughter, as his wife also."* (vss.26-28) Jacob did not have to wait another seven years to be given Rachel. She was given to him as soon as he agreed to serve Laban another seven years. Jacob had already served Laban seven years for Rachel. But now he would have to serve another seven years to *"fulfill"* Leah's *"week."* We are told, *"And he went in also unto Rachel,…and served with him yet seven other years."* (vs.30) Jacob was told to *"fulfill her week"* and he did so and served Laban *"yet seven other years."* Therefore, we can see how a week is representative of seven years.

We now know that a *"week"* in God's prophetic calendar of time represents seven years. So, if we are told *"Seventy weeks"* are determined on Daniel's people and upon his Holy city, then we must understand it to be representative of a total of 490 years.

Israel has hardened her heart against God. They have rebelled against God since the beginning. They rebelled against Moses and all others who tried to lead them in the ways of the Lord. Israel rejected Jesus as the Messiah and in so doing was broken off in unbelief from God's favor as a nation. God will not receive them again until the time of Christ's Second Coming to the earth, at which time Israel will then know and understand that Jesus **is** the Messiah. This is not to say that God does not protect Israel today. He does protect Israel to a certain degree, just as He does America and other countries.

When Jesus died upon the cross He became the atonement for sin for the entire world. But Israel has not yet taken steps to accept Jesus as Savior or Messiah. Therefore, they will not return to Christ until the Second Coming, at which time Jesus will *"make an end of sins"* and *"make reconciliation for iniquity"* and *"bring in everlasting righteousness."* Then will Israel's eyes be opened and they will repent and turn their hearts to God.

"Know therefore and understand, that from the going forth of the commandment to restore and to build Jerusalem unto Messiah, the Prince, shall be seven weeks, and threescore and two weeks..." (Dan.9:25)

By using the same principle as earlier, we can determine the meaning of the *"seven weeks, and threescore and two weeks."* We know that each of these *"weeks"* represent seven years. Therefore, the *"seven weeks,"* literally seven weeks of seven years, would equal to a total of 49 years. We are told that *"from the going forth of the commandment to restore and to build Jerusalem"* until the time that Jerusalem was finally rebuilt, a period of 49 years took place.

There were three decrees that actually went forth concerning the rebuilding of Jerusalem. The first decree was given during the time of King Cyrus, who was King of Persia. (See Ezra 1:1-4) After Cyrus, two other kings had succeeded him. His son, Cambyses, became king of Persia for a period of seven years. During his reign, work on the temple and city ceased. (Ezra 4:1-24) The second king was Darius I. Work did not continue on the temple or the city of Jerusalem until the second year of the reign of Darius II, who was the third king to follow Cyrus. (Ezra 4:24 Amp.) This was when the second decree was issued. Cyrus issued the first decree approximately seventeen or eighteen years before Darius II issued the second decree. Artaxerxes issued the third and final decree in the *"month of Nisan, in the twentieth year"* of his reign. (Neh. 2:1-8) It took 49 years to finish rebuilding the city of Jerusalem after the third and final decree was issued, which was given about the year 450 BC.

There have been many who have differed on the year when the final decree was issued. Some believe it was in about the year 445 BC, while others think it may have been in about the year 452 BC. We know that Jesus was approximately 33 years of age when He was crucified. Therefore, if we were to subtract His age of 33 from the 483 years, which is the length of time from the *"commandment to restore and build Jerusalem..."* unto the time we are told *"shall Messiah be cut off,"* which is a reference to His death on the cross, we would find that the approximate year that the final decree was issued would be 450 BC.

The *"threescore and two weeks"* in this verse represent a period of 434 years. This is arrived at by understanding that the *"threescore and two weeks"* actually mean 62 weeks. So, again, we must understand that these 62 weeks are weeks of years. We can see this in 2 Chron. 36:21 where we are told *"the land had enjoyed her sabbaths; for as long as she lay desolate she kept sabbath, to fulfill threescore and ten years."* I spoke of this earlier about Israel being enslaved and ruled in other parts of the world for a period of *"seventy years."* (Jer. 25:11) This *"threescore and ten years"* are the same as the *"seventy years."* Thus, if we multiply the 62 weeks by seven years, we get a total of 434 years. This 62-week period began immediately after the first period of 49 years, and ends at the death of *"Messiah, the Prince."* Therefore, *"from the going forth of the commandment to restore and build Jerusalem unto the Messiah, the Prince, shall be"* 483 years. The 49 years and the 434 years add to a total of 483 years.

"...after threescore and two weeks shall Messiah be cut off" (Dan. 9:26)

This is not a second set of 62 weeks. It is the same 62 weeks as in the previous verse. Daniel 9: 25 and 26 should say, *"from the going forth of the commandment to restore and build Jerusalem unto Messiah, the Prince, shall be 483 years. After that shall Messiah be cut off."* The term *"cut off,"* as stated earlier, is in reference to the death of Jesus on the cross. Therefore, when Jesus died on the cross at the approximate age of 33 years, a total of 483 years had elapsed since the decree was issued to restore and build Jerusalem.

If 483 years are now completed, and a total of 490 years were *"determined"* upon Daniel's people and his holy city, then only seven years yet remains to be fulfilled. It was not fulfilled within seven years after Jesus' death on the cross. It is still not fulfilled. It is a future period of time that is yet to be fulfilled. You may ask, what about the time from Jesus' death on the cross till now? What is this period of time? This is the period of time known as the Church Age. This period of time is parenthetical to the normal flow of this prophecy. The Church Age began after Jesus died upon the cross and will continue until Jesus comes to Rapture the Church.

As you can see, the Church was not a part of the first 483 years of this prophecy, and it **will not** be a part of the last seven years of this prophecy. The Church is not Daniel's people and it certainly is not his holy city.

Therefore, the prophecy **cannot** include the Church Age, in which we now live. The last week, or the seventieth week, the last seven years of this prophecy, will not begin until the Church is taken out of the earth. When the Church is taken out, and the *"man of sin"* is revealed (2 Thess. 2:3) and he enters into a covenant, or peace agreement with Israel for a period of seven years (Dan. 9:27), THEN will the last seven years of this prophecy begin.

The events that will take place during the final seven years of the prophecy of the Seventy Weeks will be discussed in a later chapter. But first, the event that must take place BEFORE this final seven-year period can begin will be discussed. It is the greatest event that is yet future and must be fulfilled before the seventieth week can begin. It is the event that is called the Rapture of the Church. This event can happen at any time. Currently, with all that is going on in the world, it is only a matter of WHEN Jesus will return, and how soon. Are you watching and ready for His return? We are told to *"Watch, therefore; for ye know not what hour your Lord doth come."* (St. Matt. 24:42)

Are there any prophecies that yet need to be fulfilled before the Rapture can take place? No. Jesus can come at any moment. However, there are some events that the Bible tells us about that do need to come into place. Whether or not they will come into place before the Rapture is unknown. If they do not, this means nothing. They can very rapidly fall into place after the Rapture and the Bible still be correct.

The Church could very possibly still be on earth when Antichrist comes into power of one of the ten kingdoms of the Revised Roman Empire. The nations that are now within the old Roman Empire will soon become ten kingdoms and become the Revised Roman Empire. Whether they will be called the Revised Roman Empire or not is neither here nor there. But for this study, I will call them the Revised Roman Empire.

We are told in Daniel 7:7 that Daniel had seen in *"night visions,…a fourth beast,…and it had ten horns."* The prior three *"beasts"* that he had seen represented certain kingdoms. The first *"beast was like a lion, and had eagle's wings."* (vs. 4) This was representative of the Babylonian Empire. The second *"beast"* was *"like a bear,"* (vs. 5) and it was representative of the Medo-Persian Empire that followed the Babylonian Empire. Daniel then saw a third *"beast"* that was *"like a leopard,"* which was representative of the Grecian Empire that followed the Medo-Persian Empire. We have all read about these different empires in our history books in school. Then Daniel saw this *"fourth beast,"* which is representative of the old Roman Empire. He said it had *"ten horns."* These *"ten horns"* represented the ten kingdoms within the old Roman Empire.

Now, look at verse 8. Daniel says, *"I considered the horns, and, behold, there came up among them another little horn, before which there were three of the first horns plucked up by the roots."* The vision now has become a vision of the end-time. In order for the Revised Roman Empire to become a reality, something must happen to make it so. Possibly an agreement between all the nations that make up the area within the old Roman Empire will come into being that will cause them to become ten kingdoms? Perhaps a war will break out, and when it is over, these nations will become the ten kingdoms. At any rate, when these ten kingdoms are formed, they will become the Revised Roman Empire. Out of one of these kingdoms, one will rise up against three other kingdoms within the empire and will wage war against them. This *"little horn"* will *"subdue three kings."* (Dan. 7:24)

From where does this *"little horn"* come? Who is he? The Bible gives us the answer in chapter 8 of Daniel. In this chapter, Daniel sees a vision of a *"ram"* and a *"he-goat."* These two engage in battle and eventually the *"he-goat"* becomes the victor. In verses 20 and 21 we are told who these are. The *"ram"* is the *"kings of Media and Persia."* Therefore, the *"ram"* is representative of the Medo-Persian Empire just as was the *"bear"* earlier. Then the *"he-goat"* must represent *"the king of Greece"* just as did the *"leopard"* in the earlier vision. However, in verse 21 we are told that *"the great horn that is between his eyes is the first king."* This was none other than Alexander the Great, which we also learned about in our history books in school. When Alexander the Great died, his kingdom, the Grecian Empire, was divided among his four Generals. *"Now that being broken, whereas four stood up for it, four kingdoms shall stand up out of the nation, but not in his power."* (Vs.22) Therefore, the Grecian Empire was divided and became four kingdoms, i.e. Syria, Turkey, Egypt and Greece. This is a foreshadowing of the yet future *"beast"* that shall rise up out of the Revised Roman Empire.

When the ten kingdoms of the Revised Roman Empire become actuality, then the *"little horn"* of Dan. 8:9, and the *"beast"* of Rev. 13:1 will rise up and wage war against three of the ten kingdoms within the Revised Roman Empire. I believe that this *"beast"* will come from Syria, which is the Northern Kingdom of the old Grecian Empire. We are told that *"at the time of the end shall the king of the south push at him; and the king of the north shall come against him like a whirlwind,…and he shall enter into the countries, and shall overflow and pass through."* (Dan. 11:40) The king of the south is the king of Egypt and they will war against each other. In doing so, the kings of Greece and Turkey will ally themselves with Egypt. We are told the *"little horn"* will *"subdue three kings."* (Remember, the old Grecian Empire was divided into four kingdoms.) Therefore, it is my belief that the King of Syria will war against the kingdoms of Egypt, Turkey, and Greece, and he will become victor over them and become ruler over all of the old Grecian empire.

The Church could possibly still be on earth during the time of the forming of the Revised Roman Empire. It is a very good possibility that as soon as these ten kingdoms are formed together, then Antichrist, the *"little horn,"* will make a covenant with Israel to perhaps protect them so they can rebuild the temple and renew their worshipping. It is very unlikely that the Church will be on the earth after this *"covenant"* is made. It is also very unlikely that the Church will be on the earth during the war that the *"little horn"* is waging against the kingdoms of Egypt, Greece, and Turkey, since this war will be an ongoing war during the first half of the Tribulation period.

Chapter Two
THE RAPTURE OF THE CHURCH

The period of time from the crucifixion of Christ unto the present is known as the "Church Age." This period of time is parenthetical to the normal flow of time of the prophecy of the *"Seventy weeks"* that was discussed in the first chapter. The Church was not a part of the first 69 weeks of this prophecy, nor will it be a part of the seventieth week. The Church is in no way a part of any of the prophecy of the *"Seventy weeks"* spoken of in Daniel 9:24.

To clarify the term "Rapture," Webster's Dictionary defines it as *"to carry or to snatch away from."* In 1Thess. 4:17 we are told that we *"shall be caught up"* to be with Jesus! This is virtually a *"snatching away"* from this earth to meet Jesus *"in the air."* We are told that the *"dead in Christ shall rise first: Then we who are alive and remain shall be caught up together with them in the clouds, to meet the Lord in the air; and so shall we ever be with the Lord."* Therefore, no grave shall prevent those who are Christ's from coming out of the ground and going up to meet with Jesus! Gravity will lose its grip on those who belong to Jesus and who yet remain alive on the earth, and they, too, will rise to meet with Him! This is the Rapture of the Church!

As stated earlier, there are no prophecies that yet need to be fulfilled before the Rapture can take place. Jesus can come to gather His people unto Himself at any moment. As Christians we need to be ready and watching for the moment that He returns. He **will** come again! When, no one knows. However, we must continue to live our lives in expectation of His soon return.

A. Prophecies of The Rapture

There are several scriptures throughout the Bible that predict the Rapture of the Church. The Rapture of the Church should not be confused with the Second Coming of Christ to the earth. During the Rapture, Jesus will not come to the earth. He will, however, come *"in the air"* and He will gather His people together and they will be *"caught up"* to *"meet him"* and forever *"be with the Lord."* (1 Thess. 4:17) At the time of Jesus' Second Coming, it will be to the earth, where He will *"stand in that day upon the Mount of Olives, which is before Jerusalem on the east."* (Zech. 14:4) He will come to take His place as *"king over all the earth,"* (Zech. 14:9) and to establish His kingdom upon the earth. (Zech. 14:9-11)

Let us look at some of the prophecies of Jesus' coming to Rapture the Church.

"Let not your heart be troubled; ye believe in God, believe also in me. In my Father's house are many mansions; if it were not so, I would have told you. I go to prepare a place for you. And if I go and prepare a place for you, I will come again, and receive you unto myself, that where I am, there ye may be also." (St. John 14:1-3)

"And when he had spoken these things, while they beheld, he was taken up; and a cloud received him out of their sight. And while they looked steadfastly toward heaven as he went up, behold, two men stood by them in white apparel; which also said, ye men of Galilee, why stand ye gazing up into heaven? This same Jesus, which is taken up from you into heaven shall so come in like manner as ye have seen him go into heaven." (Acts 1:9-11)

"For if we believe that Jesus died and rose again, even so them also who sleep in Jesus will God bring with him. For this we say unto you by the word of the Lord, that we who are alive and remain unto the coming of the Lord shall not precede them who are asleep. For the Lord himself shall descend from heaven with a shout, with the voice of the Archangel, and with the trump of God; and the dead in Christ shall rise first; then we who are alive and remain shall be caught up together with them in the clouds, to meet the Lord in the air; and so shall we ever be with the Lord. Wherefore, comfort one another with these words." (1 Thess. 4:14-18)

"Watch, therefore; for ye know not what hour your Lord doth come." (St. Matt. 24:42)

"Behold, I shew you a mystery; we shall not all sleep, but we shall all be changed, In a moment, in the twinkling of an eye, at the last trump; for the trumpet shall sound, and the dead shall be raised incorruptible, and we shall be changed. For this corruptible must put on incorruption, and this mortal must put on immortality." (1 Cor. 15:51-53)

"For God hath not appointed us to wrath, but to obtain salvation by our Lord Jesus Christ." (1 Thess. 5:9)

"Because thou hast kept the word of my patience, I will also keep thee from the hour of temptation, which shall come upon all the world, to try them that dwell upon the earth." (Rev. 3:10)

"But of that day and hour knoweth no man, no, not the angels of heaven, but my Father only." (St. Matt. 24:36)

These are only a few of the scriptures that tell us that Jesus will come to Rapture the Church. We can rest assured that at some point in time unknown to us, Jesus **will** come. We are told that He will come with a *"shout"* and with *"the voice of the*

Archangel." One can only imagine what the *"shout"* will be, but, I can just hear Him shouting, "Arise! Come up here!" When the *"trump of God"* is sounded, it will wake those who are asleep *"in Jesus,"* and *"in a moment, in the twinkling of an eye"* they will be changed. Those who are *"alive and remain"* will also hear this shout and the blast of the trumpet, and they, too, will be instantly changed. We are told the *"corruptible must put on incorruption, and the mortal must put on immortality."* Thank God that no grave will be able to keep the saint of God in the ground! Gravity on this earth will not have the power to keep the saints, who hear that trumpet sound, from leaving this earth to meet Jesus *"in the air."*

We are warned that we are to *"Watch, therefore; for ye know not what hour your Lord doth come."* (St. Matt. 24:42) Also, we are further warned that *"of that day and hour knoweth no man, no, not the angels of heaven, but my Father only."* (St. Matt. 24:36) Jesus wants us to be watching and ready for His return. In St. Matt. 25:1-13, we are given the parable of the *"ten virgins."* Five of these virgins were wise to have their *"lamps"* full of oil and extra *"oil in their vessels."* The remaining five virgins took their lamps, but did not bring extra oil. While the ten were waiting, they *"slumbered and slept."* Suddenly the *"cry,"* or the trumpet sounded, and they all arose and trimmed their lamps. Those that had extra oil were ready and prepared to meet with the *"Bridegroom."* The *"foolish virgins"* wanted to get some oil from the wise virgins because their lamps had gone out and they had no more oil. They were told to go and buy extra oil, lest there not be enough for them all. So while the *"foolish virgins"* were gone to buy oil, the *"Bridegroom"* came and *"they that were ready went in with him to the marriage; and the door was shut."* (St. Matt: 25:10) When the *"foolish virgins"* returned, they said, *"Lord, Lord, open to us. But he answered and said, Verily I say unto you, I know you not."* (vs. 11,12) This is a picture of the time when Jesus will come to gather His children from this earth and take them to be with Him. Those who are watching and who are ready will go to be with Him. Those who are perhaps watching, but not ready, will not be able to enter into the marriage. They will be left behind on this earth to endure the *"hour of temptation, which shall come upon all the world, to try them that dwell upon the earth."* (Rev. 3:10)

At the time of the Rapture of the Church, there will be great chaos on the earth. One can imagine the hysteria and turmoil that will take place. Saints who are taken away will have suddenly disappeared from before the eyes of those left behind. All different modes of transportation will have operators who are suddenly *"caught up"* to be with Jesus, and those vehicles, trains, planes, buses, trucks, boats; every mode of transportation, will suddenly be without operators and they will all crash. Many of those who are left behind will suddenly lose their lives and be lost forever. It will be like in the days of Noah, when God told him to build the ark. People were going about doing their own things, and living like life would never end. They probably laughed at Noah and mocked him for building the ark. But when the rains began and the floods came, the people probably begged Noah to open the door of the ark to them. But they perished in the flood. Those who are not ready for Jesus' coming to Rapture the Church will know that they were left behind.

If you are not ready, or you are unsure, now is the time to get ready for Jesus' return. May I ask that you take the time now and ask Jesus to come into your heart today? He stands at the door of your heart and knocks. (Rev. 3:20) If you will ask Him to come into your heart, He will come! You CAN be ready for His return.

B. The Purpose of The Rapture

"For we all must appear before the judgment seat of Christ; that everyone may receive the things done in his body, according to that he hath done, whether it be good or bad." (2 Cor. 5:10)

"For the mystery of iniquity doth already work; only he who now hindereth will continue to hinder until he be taken out of the way." (2 Thess. 2:7)

The purpose of the Rapture of the Church is two-fold. We are told that *"we must all appear before the judgment seat of Christ."* This judgment is not to judge the saints for the sins in their lives. It is to *"test every man's work of what sort it is."* (1 Cor. 3:13) When we become Christians, our sins are judged at the time of our casting our sins upon God. This is not to say that we do not sin as Christians. But we are told that if we do sin, we have *"an advocate with the Father, Jesus Christ the righteous."* (1 John 2:1) Therefore, if any man sins, he can receive forgiveness and continue on in his Christian walk. No, this appearance before the *"judgment seat of Christ"* is for the testing, or judging, of our works that we have done while in the body as Christians. It will be at this judgment where those whose *"works"* that are tested, will receive their rewards, or *"suffer loss."* (1 Cor. 3:15) Those whose *"works"* survive the test will receive a reward. But if their *"works"* do not survive, and are *"burned up"* by the fire, they will *"suffer loss."* (This subject will be discussed in more detail in the next chapter.)

The second purpose of the Rapture of the Church, we are told, is that *"only he that now hindereth will continue to hinder until he be taken out of the way."* (2 Thess. 2:7) Who is this that *"hinders?"* Could it be the Church? The Church is definitely the one who hinders! The Holy Spirit is within the Church. Every person who becomes a child of God is endowed with the Holy Spirit to a certain degree. Others have received the in-filling of the Holy Spirit such as those at Pentecost were. (Acts 2:1-4) It is the Holy Spirit that holds at bay Satan and all his evil work. Satan is able to do a lot today, but when the Holy Spirit is *"taken out of the way,"* he will go rampant. When the Holy Spirit is *"taken out of the way,"* then sin will abound in such a manner as never was experienced at any other time on the earth. Antichrist will be endowed with satanic power and Satan will spread his evil the world over.

The fact that the Holy Spirit will be *"taken out of the way"* at the time of the Rapture is not to say that it will be removed entirely. The scripture says that it will *"be taken out of the way,"* perhaps meaning that the Holy Spirit will step aside to allow Satan to do his evil work. It is the Holy Spirit that woos and causes us to come to Jesus. We are told that there will be those who will become born again believers during the Tribulation period. (Rev. 7) Therefore, the Holy Spirit **will** do a work during this period of time.

C. How To Prepare For The Rapture

The Bible teaches that there are several ways in which we can become prepared to meet Jesus at the time of the Rapture. Following are a few instructions that we can follow that will prepare us for this event.

1. We Must Go To Church

"Not forsaking the assembling of ourselves together, as the manner of some is, but exhorting one another, and so much the more, as ye see the day approaching." (Heb. 10: 25)

2. We Must Partake Of The Lord's Supper

"For as often as ye eat the bread, and drink this cup, ye do show the Lord's death till He come." (1 Cor. 11: 26)

3. We Must Be Patient

"Be ye also patient, establish you hearts; for the coming of the Lord draweth near." (James 5: 8)

4. We Must Love One Another

"And the Lord make you to increase and abound in love one toward another, and toward all men, even as we do toward you, To the end he may establish your hearts unblamable in holiness before God, even our Father, at the coming of our Lord Jesus Christ with all his saints." (1 Thess. 3: 12, 13)

5. We Must Live A Separated Life

"...For we are the temple of the living God....Therefore come out from among them and be separate, says the Lord. Touch no unclean thing and I will receive you." (2 Cor. 6: 16-17 NIV)

"Beloved, now are we the sons of God, and it doth not yet appear what we shall be, but we know that, when he shall appear, we shall be like him; for we shall see him as he is. And every man that hath this hope in him purifieth himself even as he is pure." (1 John 3: 2, 3)

"Teaching us that, denying ungodliness and worldly lusts, we should live soberly, righteously, and godly, in this present age. Looking for that blessed hope, and the glorious appearing of the great God and our Savior, Jesus Christ." (Titus 2: 12, 13)

For further instructions, please read 1 Cor. 4: 5; 2 Tim. 4: 1, 2; 1 Pet. 5: 2, 4; Jude 21-23; Col. 3: 1-25.

D. Who Will Be *"Caught Up"* In The Rapture?

Those who will be *"caught up"* at the time of the Rapture will be those that have their sins covered by the blood of Jesus. From the time of Jesus' death upon the cross till the day of the Rapture, this period of time is called the Church Age. It will be these saints of this age that will be *"caught up."* Every child of God should be watching and ready for that glorious day! We are looking forward to the day when we will have a new heaven and a new earth which is *"the home of righteousness. So then, dear friends, since you are looking forward to this, make every effort to be found spotless, blameless and at peace with him."* (2 Pet. 3: 13-14 NIV) Therefore, it will be the saints of the Church Age that will be "caught up" at the time of the Rapture.

What about the Old Testament saints? **They have already been resurrected.** We see this in St. Matt. 27:51-53, where we are told that after Jesus' death upon the cross, the *"graves were opened; and many bodies of the saints that slept were raised."* These did not continue to live on the earth and then die again and get buried again. They were resurrected with Jesus. The fact that they were seen by *"many"* is proof that they were raised from the dead.

Jesus is first in resurrection. (Col. 1:18; Rev. 1:5) Although these graves are said to have opened at the time of Jesus' death on the cross, it was after He was raised from death that these saints were raised from the dead. We are told, *"When he ascended on high, he led captives in his train…"* (Eph. 4:8 NIV) Therefore, these *"captive"* are the saints of the Old Testament. Jesus said to the thief while on the cross, *"today you will be with me in paradise."* (St. Luke 23:43 NIV)

After Jesus died, we are told that He went to the lower parts of the earth, (Eph. 4:9) and it was at this time that He liberated the Old Testament saints. When Jesus was raised from the dead, so were the Old Testament saints. They, along with the thief on the cross, went with Jesus to *"paradise."* Therefore, the Old Testament saints are already resurrected and they are waiting for the time when Jesus will return to resurrect, or Rapture, the saints of this, the Church Age.

E. The Result Of The Rapture

At the time of the Rapture of the Church, there will be mass confusion on the part of those left on the earth. People will wonder with amazement of the strange disappearances of millions of people throughout the world. Those left behind, who once knew the Lord as Savior and who were in a sinful condition at the time of the Rapture will know they were left behind and many will return to God.

Furthermore, the result of the Rapture will be the ushering in of the Tribulation Period. It will be the beginning of the end. It will be the close of a long journey for the saints of the Church Age.

The most tragic result will be that there will be so many that will be left behind to endure the trials during the Tribulation period. This does not have to happen. As Christians today, we can work to gain many others into the house of God. There is much to do, many who need to be saved. We are told to *"occupy till I come."* (St. Luke 19:13) That doesn't mean that we should just sit around and wait for Jesus' coming. As Christians, we need to be about the Father's business. We need to be working to win the lost to Christ.

Chapter Three
PARENTHETIC—THE JUDGMENT SEAT OF CHRIST

After the Rapture of the Church, there are certain events that will take place in Heaven. While the Tribulation period is beginning to get under way on earth, these heavenly scenes will unfold. The first of these scenes will be the Judgment Seat of Christ. In this chapter this event will be discussed thoroughly. Other heavenly events will be discussed in a later chapter.

Once the Rapture of the Church is completed, the saints will be in the presence of Jesus. A lot of people have the idea that once a Christian leaves this earth, he will have to stand in judgment for the sins he committed while in this life. But this is not true. The fact is that once we become born-again believers, the blood of Jesus has washed away the sins we once had. We are told that our sins will never be remembered. The following verses of scripture assure us that once we surrender our lives to God, we will never be judged for our sins.

"For as high as the heavens are above the earth, so great is his love for those who fear him; as far as the east is from the west, so far has he removed our transgressions from us." (Ps. 103:11-12 NIV)

"...thou hast in love to my soul delivered it from the pit of corruption; for thou hast cast all my sins behind thy back." (Isa. 38:17)

"I, even I, am he who blots out your transgressions, for my own sake, and remembers your sins no more." (Isa. 43:25 NIV)

"I have swept away your offenses like a cloud, your sins like the morning mist. Return to me, for I have redeemed you." (Isa. 44:22 NIV)

"...for I will forgive their iniquity, and I will remember their sin no more." (Jer. 31:34)

"Who is a God like you, who pardons sin and forgives the transgression of the remnant of his inheritance? You do not stay angry forever but delight to show mercy. You will again have compassion on us; you will tread our sins underfoot and hurl all our iniquities into the depths of the sea." (Mic. 7:18-19 NIV)

"For God did not send the Son into the world in order to judge— to reject, to condemn, to pass sentence on—the world; but that the world might find salvation and be made safe and sound through Him. He who believes on Him—who clings to, trusts in, relies on Him—is not judged (he who trusts in Him never comes up for judgement; for him there is no rejection, no condemnation; he incurs no damnation). But he who does not believe (not cleave to, rely on, trust in Him) is judged already; (he has already been convicted; has already received his sentence) because he has not believed on and trusted in the name of the only begotten Son of God.—He is condemned for refusing to let his trust rest in Christ's name." (St. John 3:17-18 Amplified Bible)

"But if we walk in the light, as he is in the light, we have fellowship with one another, and the blood of Jesus, his Son, purifies us from all sin." (1 John 1:7 NIV)

At the time of our rebirth into the family of God, we became judged. Our sins were immediately cast away *"as far as the east is from the west."* God will never again remember our sins! He has *"swept away your offenses like a cloud, your sins like the morning mist."* He **cannot** and **will not** remember *"your sins."*

This is not to say that a child of God cannot commit sins. He can sin at any time, and many do. However, we do not have to dwell in that sin. We are told that *"if anybody does sin, we have one who speaks to the Father in our defense—Jesus Christ, the Righteous One."* (1 John 2:1 NIV) Therefore, if a child of God does commit a sin, he can go to the Father, and confess that sin, and Jesus, Who is our *"Advocate,"* will speak to the Father in our defense. From that point on, you are free from sin, and that sin has been judged.

Many people make the mistake in thinking that if they commit a wrong deed, or commit some sin, whether it is a small sin or a large one, then they have lost their salvation. The truth of the matter is that this is a lie of the enemy! If you make a mistake, all you need do is to go to the Father and confess to Him your sin. We are told, *"If we say we have no sin, we deceive ourselves, and the truth is not in us. If we confess our sins, he is faithful and just to forgive us our sins, and to cleanse us from all unrighteousness."* (1 John 1:8-9) So there is no need to linger in a sinful condition when you do commit a sin. Just confess that sin to God, ask for His forgiveness and get on with your Christian walk! The sooner you do this, the better off you will be. The Holy Spirit will grieve within you until you both confess the sin to God and ask His forgiveness, or until you just totally ignore the Spirit and He leaves. But no Christian should believe that if he commits a sin, he is lost. He only needs to confess that sin to God and ask for forgiveness, and then get on with his life.

On the other hand, if a Christian sins and does not go to the

Father and confess that sin, he **can** fall by the wayside. As long as you have sin in your life and do not bring it to God and ask for His forgiveness, you'll not live a productive life for God. You will have deceived yourself into thinking that all is fine even though you still have some small sin. This is the way carnal Christians live. As long as you have any sin in your life, you will not please God! The Word of God tells us that *"If we deliberately keep on sinning after we have received the knowledge of the truth, no sacrifice for sins is left, but only a fearful expectation of judgment and of raging fire that will consume the enemies of God."* (Heb. 10:26-27 NIV) As long as there is sin in your life, you *will not* enter into the kingdom of Heaven! You will be one of the many who are left behind at the time of the Rapture. Also, this you should know. If you die with sin in your life, **you will be eternally lost**! If you think that having one small sin in your life is alright and that you will still be able to go to Heaven, you are very sadly mistaken. **No sin** will enter into the Kingdom of Heaven! *"He that committeth sin is of the devil; for the devil sinneth from the beginning. For this purpose the Son of God was manifested. That he might destroy the works of the devil."* (1 John 3:8)

If a person who has once known Jesus as Lord and Savior commits sin and turns their heart away from God, they will be doomed to Hell. Unless they confess the sins they have committed, and continue their walk with Christ, they will not be ready for Jesus' coming. We are told, *"But because of your stubbornness and your unrepentant heart, you are storing up wrath against yourself for the day of God's wrath, when his righteous judgment will be revealed. God will give to each person according to what he has done....For God does not show favoritism."* (Rom. 2:5-6, 11 NIV) Therefore, we all **will** be judged. Either we are judged when we repent, or we will be judged on the day of God's judgment of the sinners. For the child of God who has repented of every sin, there is no wrath of God. That person will, as long as he is free from sin, be *"caught up"* to be with

Jesus and then it will be his *"works"* that will be judged at the Judgment Seat of Christ, not his sins.

Those who do not believe, or do not become born again into the family of God have *"already been convicted; has already received his sentence."* How can we say this? Because it is written in God's Word! We are told that those who refuse to believe in Jesus, who refuse to make Him Lord and Savior in their lives, *"is judged already;....He is condemned for refusing to let his trust rest in Christ's name."* For the unbeliever, the one who never allows Jesus to become his Lord and Savior, he is already sentenced to spend eternity separated from God. Unless the unbeliever repents and asks Jesus to become his Lord and Savior, he will spend eternity in *"the lake of fire."* (Rev. 20:11-15)

If you have never asked Jesus to come into your life, you can do so now. If you are not sure of your salvation, you too can really know without a doubt that Jesus is your Lord and Savior. I would like to take this opportunity to ask that if you are not a believer, or perhaps you are unsure of whether you are truly saved or not, will you now ask Jesus to come into your heart? All you need to do is confess that you are a sinner and repent of all your sins. The word "repent" simply means to have a change of heart. To repent means that you will change the way you believe and the way you act. If you do this now, you will be free from the judgment that will come upon the wicked. You will be among the believers of God and of His Christ, and you will never be judged again for any sins. You will join the millions of believers that will someday hear the trumpet of God and rise to meet Jesus in the air! Will you ask Jesus to become Lord and Savior of your life today?

A. The Purpose of the Judgment Seat of Christ

"For we must all appear before the judgment seat of Christ, that everyone may receive the things done in his body, according to that he hath done, whether it be good or bad." (2 Cor. 5:10)

"For we are laborers together with God; ye are God's cultivated field, ye are God's building." (1 Cor. 3:9)

"What? Know ye not that your body is the temple of the Holy Spirit who is in you, whom ye have of God, and ye are not your own? For ye are bought with a price; therefore, glorify God in your body and in your spirit, which are God's." (1 Cor. 6:19-20)

"And ye are Christ's, and Christ is God's." (1 Cor. 3:23)

"If any man builds on this foundation using gold, silver, costly stones, wood, hay or straw, his work will be shown for what it is, because the Day will bring it to light. It will be revealed with fire, and the fire will test the quality of each man's work. If what he has built survives, he will receive his reward. If it is burned up, he will suffer loss; he himself will be saved, but only as one escaping through the flames." (1 Cor. 3:12-15 NIV)

As children of God, we are *"bought with a price."* We belong to God. We are told that we are *"laborers together with God"* and that we *"are God's cultivated field."* The work that we do as Christians is the material that we use to build on the *"foundation."* We do not know how God will determine what works will be categorized as *"gold, silver, costly stones"* or what will be considered *"wood, hay or straw."* But we can know that the material that is considered *"gold, silver, costly stones"* will most likely be the *"good"* works and that they will survive the *"test"* by fire. But the *"wood, hay or straw"* will most likely be the *"bad"* works and will be consumed or *"burned up."* We are told that those whose works survive the test will *"receive his reward."* And those whose works are *"burned up"* will *"suffer loss,"* but *"he himself will be saved, but only as one escaping through the flames."*

We are told that *"we must all appear before the judgment seat of Christ, that each may receive what is due him for the things done while in the body, whether good or bad."* (2 Cor. 5:10 NIV) Then we have the account of 1 Cor. 3:11-16 where we are given the measure by how our works are to be tested. As stated earlier, those whose *"works"* survive the testing will *"receive his reward."* Those that would *"suffer loss"* was also mentioned. We are not told what this *"loss"* will be, but it very well could be the loss of a crown reward. However, although some will *"suffer loss,"* they will be saved, *"but only as one escaping through the flames."* (1 Cor. 3:15 NIV) But **all** that appear before the judgment seat of Christ will receive robes. They will be *"arrayed in fine linen, clean and white."* (Rev. 19:8) They will be presented to Jesus to become His bride! These are the Church, who will be presented *"as a radiant church without stain or wrinkle or any other blemish, but holy and blameless."* (Eph. 5:27 NIV) (The bride of Christ, therefore, cannot be any other group other than the Church.) As stated earlier, the Old Testament saints were not a part of the Church, for the Church Age began after Jesus died on the cross, and ends with His coming to Rapture the Church. Furthermore, the saints of the Tribulation period will not be a part of the Church, because the Church is already taken to be with Jesus before the beginning of the Tribulation period.

"Therefore, my dear brothers, stand firm. Let nothing move you. Always give yourselves fully to the work of the Lord, because you know that your labor in the Lord is not in vain." (1 Cor. 15:58 NIV)

Don't give up and don't give in to the enemy when he tries to make you fall. If you will continue to work and stand firm, letting nothing move you, but always giving of yourselves fully to the work of the Lord, you will stand for Jesus and know that your work will survive the test. You **will** receive your reward!

There are a lot of areas of interest in which we can work to please God. In the following, it could be that these are a few of the works which will be decided as to whether they will be placed in the *"good"* works or *"bad"* works category.

1. How We Treat Other Believers

"God is not unjust; he will not forget your work and the love you have shown him as you have helped his people and continue to help them." (Heb. 6:10 NIV)

How do you treat other believers? Do you ignore their needs and their desires? As Christians, we need to be sensitive to the Spirit and be willing to help other Christians. Do you pray for Christians who are sick, or in financial distress? Do you pray for the desires and needs of your fellow Christians? Each child of God has certain desires and needs and as Christians, we need to pray for each other that those desires and needs are fulfilled. We should never fail to be willing to listen and to pray for our fellow Christians.

2. By Paying Tithes

"Bring all the tithes into the storehouse, that there may be food in mine house…" (Mal. 3:10)

"On the first day of every week, each one of you should set aside a sum of money in keeping with his income, saving it up, so that when I come no collections will have to be made." (1 Cor. 16:2 NIV)

Every child of God should to pay his tithes. What are the tithes? The tithe is the first ten-percent to be taken off of what you earn or receive, and this belongs to God. We are asked, *"Will a man rob God?"* (Mal. 3:8) When we do not pay the tithe, we rob God! When we pay our tithes we are giving to God what belongs to Him. The tithe is His, not yours! The tithe does not necessarily have to always be monetary. You can also tithe in your time and your help. You can give clothing, food, or anything of value that you have. The important thing is that every Christian should pay the tithe.

3. Our Sufferings For Jesus

"Dear friends, do not be surprised at the painful trial you are suffering, as though something strange were happening to you. But rejoice that you participate in the sufferings of Christ, so that you may be overjoyed when his glory is revealed." (1 Pet. 4:12-13 NIV)

Every child of God, once he begins his walk with the Lord, will come under persecution of one kind or another at some point. Those that you once were friends with may suddenly decide that you aren't good enough for them. Because you no longer do the things you once did, those you once were with no longer want to be with you. As a child of God, many non-Christians may criticize you because of your faith. Jesus was also criticized and ridiculed because He was different than others. As Christians, we are to be **like** Christ. No matter what comes your way, you must continue walking with God. He will help you when the going gets rough.

4. How We Use The Gifts of God In Our Lives

"Now there are diversities of gifts, but the same Spirit." (1 Cor.12:4)

"All these are the work of one and the same Spirit, and he gives them to each one, just as he determines." (1 Cor. 12:11 NIV)

"For this reason I remind you to fan into flame the gift of God,

which is in you through the laying on of my hands." (2 Tim. 1:6 NIV)

"Each one should use whatever gift he has received to serve others. Faithfully administering God's grace in its various forms." (1 Pet. 4:10 NIV) See also Heb. 3:17; 2 Cor 4:17; Ps. 90:12; James 1:2-3.)

B. The Result of The Judgment Seat of Christ

"If any man's work abide which he hath built thereupon, he shall receive a reward." (1 Cor. 3:14)

As stated earlier, it is not known what *"works"* will be placed into the good works or which will be considered the bad works. However, we do know that if we work to please God and press on toward the goal, as Paul said, *"I have fought a good fight, I have finished the course, I have kept the faith,"* (2 Tim. 3:7) we will then receive our reward. Every child of God will receive rewards at the Judgment Seat of Christ. Some, however, will *"suffer loss."* What this loss will be is unknown, but we do know that although some may suffer a loss, they will *"be saved"* because they did have works to be tested. They will not be cast into outer darkness, as some believe. Why would God allow a person to be *"caught up"* at the time of the Rapture, just to cast him into outer darkness, or into Hell, because his *"works"* were *"burned up"* at the time of testing at the Judgment Seat of Christ? God is not an unjust God! Everyone that is *"caught up"* to be with Jesus will be with Him throughout all eternity, whether his *"work"* was burned up or it survived the test.

We are told that *"If a man's work abide...he shall receive a reward."* The Bible tells us that there are certain *"crown"* rewards that will be given to believers. Paul said, *"Now there is in store for me the crown of righteousness, which the Lord, the righteous Judge, will award to me on that day—and not only to me, but also to all who have longed for his appearing."* (2 Tim. 4:8 NIV) There are other *"crown"* rewards that will be given as well. There are a total of five *"crown"* rewards.

1. The Crown of Righteousness

"Now there is in store for me the crown of righteousness…" (2 Tim.4:8 NIV)

2. The Crown of Life

"Blessed is the man who perseveres under trial, because when he has stood the test, he will receive the crown of life that God has promised to those who love him." (James 1:12 NIV)

"Do not be afraid of what you are about to suffer….Be faithful, even to the point of death, and I will give you the crown of life." (Rev. 2:10 NIV)

3. The Crown of Glory

"Be shepherds of God's flock that is under your care, serving as overseers—not because you must, but because you are willing, as God wants you to be; not greedy for money, but eager to serve; not lording it over those entrusted to you, but being examples to the flock. And when the Chief Shepherd appears, you will receive the crown of glory that will never fade away." (1 Pet. 5:2-4 NIV)

4. The Incorruptible Crown

"And every man that striveth for the mastery is temperate in all things. Now they do it to obtain a corruptible crown, but we, an incorruptible." (1 Cor. 9:25)

5. The Crown of Rejoicing

"For what is our hope, or joy, or crown of rejoicing? Are not even ye in the presence of our Lord Jesus Christ at his coming?" (1 Thess. 2:19)

These *"crown"* rewards very well could be the rewards of whose *"works"* will stand the test and survive. However, we are told that some will *"suffer loss."* Although it is not said what this *"loss"* will be, we are told that they will *"be saved, but only as one escaping through the flames."* Perhaps the *"loss"* will be that they will not receive a *"crown"* reward. Whatever the *"loss"* is, at least they will be able to enter into the joys of the Lord. Jesus tells us, *"I am coming soon. Hold on to what you have, so that no one will take your crown."* (Rev. 3:11 NIV)

Chapter Four
PARENTHETIC—THE MARRIAGE SUPPER OF THE LAMB

"Let us rejoice—and shout for joy—exulting and triumphant! Let us celebrate and ascribe to Him glory and honor, for the marriage of the Lamb (at last) has come and His bride has prepared herself. She has been permitted to dress in fine (radiant) linen—dazzling and white, for the fine linen is (signifies, represents) the righteousness— the upright, just and godly living (deeds, conduct) and right standing with God—of the saints (God's holy people). Then (the angel) said to me, Write this down: Blessed—happy, to be envied— are those who are summoned (invited, called) to the marriage supper of the Lamb. And he said to me (further), These are the true words— the genuine and exact declarations—of God." (Rev. 19: 7-9 Amp.)

After the Church has been *"caught up"* to be with Jesus, and after the testing of the *"works"* at the Judgment Seat of Christ is completed, the next event for the Church is the marriage of the Lamb. After the marriage, a banquet will be held, which is the marriage supper. Who are these that are being married? Who is the bridegroom and who is the bride? Who will be the guests at this wedding and at the supper? Jesus is the bridegroom and the Church will be the bride. The guests will be the Old Testament and Tribulation saints.

A. The Bridegroom

During Jesus' ministry, He referred unto Himself as the bridegroom on several occasions. In St. Matthews Gospel, chapter 9, the disciples of John the Baptist asked Jesus, *"How is it that we and the Pharisees fast, but your disciples do not fast?"* (vs. 14 NIV) Jesus answered them by saying, *"How can the guests of the bridegroom mourn while he is with them? The time will come when the bridegroom will be taken away from them; then they will fast."* (vs. 15 NIV) In St. Matt. 22:1-14, Jesus tells a parable of the wedding banquet. In this parable, the King's son is about to be married and the servants are sent to gather those invited to the marriage supper. It is Jesus Who is referred to as the bridegroom, or the King's son. Then in St. Matt. 25:1-10 we have the parable of the ten virgins. In this parable, Jesus again alludes to Himself as being the bridegroom. John the Baptist ascribed to Jesus as being the bridegroom when he said, *"The bride belongs to the bridegroom. The friend who attends the bridegroom waits and listens for him, and is full of joy when he hears the bridegroom's voice. That joy is mine, and it is now complete. He must become greater; I must become less."* (St. John 3:29,30 NIV) Paul illustrates that Jesus is the bridegroom in 2 Cor. 11:2 and in Eph. 5:23-32.

B. The Bride

If Jesus is the Bridegroom, then who is the bride? Again, in 2 Cor. 11:2, Paul says *"For I am jealous over you with godly jealousy; for I have espoused you to one husband that I may present you as a chaste virgin to Christ."* In Eph. 5:30-32, we are told, *"for we are members of his body....This is a profound mystery—but I am talking about Christ and the church."* The Church is the bride of Christ. It is the Church that will be *"caught up"* (1 Thess. 4:17) when Jesus comes to Rapture His saints. Therefore, it is the saints who are the body of Christ (Eph.5:30) and it is the saints who make up the body of the Church.

Some make the mistake in thinking that all believers from the beginning of time will be the bride of Christ. But this is not true. The Old Testament believers were not a part of the Church. The Church began **after** Jesus died upon the cross. All those believers who have passed on from the time of Jesus' death on the cross prior to the Rapture, and those believers who are still alive at the time of the Rapture taking place, will make up the body of the Church, which is the bride of Christ. The Old Testament saints are not the bride of Christ, which will be proved a little later.

In the Old Testament, Israel was considered the unfaithful wife of Jehovah, as referred to in Ezekiel and Hosea. She is the forsaken wife because of her adulteries, idolatries and rejection of God. Israel will someday come back to God, but she will not be the bride, for she is not considered a virgin. Israel is the unfaithful wife! A wife that is reinstated is not a virgin; therefore, Israel cannot be the bride of Christ. Jesus will receive a bride who is a virgin, and who is *"a radiant church, without stain or wrinkle or any other blemish, but holy and blameless."* (Eph. 5:27 NIV)

C. The Marriage Ceremony

Nothing is said about the marriage ceremony. We are told simply that *"the wedding of the Lamb has come."* (Rev. 19:7 NIV) One can only imagine the greatness of the wedding of Jesus and His bride. We have all seen extravagant wedding ceremonies during our lives here on earth. But I can imagine that Jesus' wedding ceremony will be much more extravagant than any wedding ceremony ever attempted on earth! And why shouldn't it be? After all, the Father is owner of all things in heaven, on earth and under the earth. He has all the most valuable of all things. His Son, Jesus, is worthy to have the best! And His bride has become worthy by virtue that she has stood the test and has stood firm and not wavered. The

Church will greatly overcome and enter into the joys of the Lord!

D. The Guests and the Marriage Supper

"Then (the angel) said to me, Write this down: Blessed—happy, to be envied—are those who are summoned (invited, called) to the marriage supper of the Lamb." (Rev. 19:9 Amp. Bible)

Who are the guests at the wedding? The guests will be the Old Testament saints and those saints of the Tribulation period. John the Baptist said, *"The bride belongs to the bridegroom. The friend who attends the bridegroom waits and listens for him, and is full of joy when he hears the bridegroom's voice. That joy is mine, and it is now complete."* (St John 3:29 NIV) John the Baptist, although he lived at the time of Jesus' life on earth, is not a part of the Church Age. He was beheaded **before** Jesus died on the cross. Therefore, he is part of the Old Testament period. He said *"the bride belongs to the bridegroom"* and he was referring to Jesus as the bridegroom. He was referring to himself and the Old Testament saints when he said *"the friend who attends the bridegroom waits and listens for him."* John the Baptist was saying that he was a friend of the bridegroom and that he had joy in that. Therefore, if John the Baptist considered himself as a friend of the bridegroom, then **all** the saints of the Old Testament before him would also fall into that category. The guests of the marriage will be the Old Testament saints and the saints of the Tribulation period.

When we read the parable of the wedding banquet in St. Matt. 22:1-13 NIV, we see that the servants of the King were sent out to gather in those invited to the banquet, or the marriage supper. But we see that the servants were refused and many of them were killed for their efforts. Then in verse 8 we are told, *"those I invited did not deserve to come."* Who are these who were invited but did not deserve to come? They are the people of Israel, the Jews. They rejected Jesus and they rejected God. They are the unfaithful wife of Jehovah! The Jews will not be the bride, as some speculate. The Jews who will return to God during the Tribulation period will, however, be a part of the guest list. We are told in verse 9, *"Go to the street corners and invite to the banquet anyone you find."* Then we are told that the servants went and *"gathered all the people they could find, both good and bad, and the wedding hall was filled with guests."* (vs.10 NIV) These are both the Jews who return to God and the gentile nations that come to know Jesus as Lord during the Tribulation period. The *"banquet hall"* will be full at the time of the marriage supper. Those who try to enter in that are not invited and who do not have on the wedding garment, which is the righteousness of God, will be cast out into outer darkness. (vs. 13)

E. The Time of the Marriage Supper of the Lamb

When will the Marriage Supper of the Lamb take place? When Jesus comes to Rapture the Church, the first thing that has to happen with those who are *"caught up"* is that they will stand before the Judgment Seat of Christ. Their *"works"* will be tested, after which, many will receive rewards. Some, as has been found, will *"suffer loss,"* but they will yet be saved. After the Judgment Seat of Christ is completed, then the wedding begins. It is my belief that the wedding will take place in heaven, whereas the marriage supper will take place on earth and coincides with the Second Coming of Jesus to the earth. I know that there will be many that will disagree with me on this one, but, nevertheless, this is the way I interpret the scriptures. It would seem to be more realistic to understand that the wedding would take place in heaven after the saints have *"made themselves ready"* and have received the garment of righteousness, which is the *"fine linen, clean and white."* (Rev. 19:8) The Church is presented as a bride who is radiant, *"without stain or wrinkle or any other blemish, but holy and blameless."* (Eph. 5:27 NIV) As stated earlier, nothing is said about the actual wedding ceremony. We are simply told that the *"wedding of the Lamb has come, and his bride has made herself ready."* (Rev. 19:7 NIV) Therefore, I submit that the actual wedding ceremony takes place in heaven. After a wedding ceremony, it is customary to have a banquet. Thus, the banquet, or the marriage supper will take place on earth at the time of Jesus' Second Coming. This will be at the close of the Tribulation period, when Jesus returns to the earth and sets up His earthly Kingdom.

Chapter Five
THE TRIBULATION PERIOD—
THE SEVENTIETH WEEK

Following the Rapture of the Church, a new period of time is introduced. This is the time known as the Tribulation period, or the Seventieth week. This Seventieth week is the final week of the prophecy of the *"Seventy weeks"* as recorded in Dan. 9:24. It has already been discovered that the first 69 weeks, or 483 years, are fulfilled. The prophecy of the *"Seventy weeks"* began in the *"month of Nisan, in the twentieth year"* of the reign of Artaxerxes, (Neh. 2:1) which was in about the year 450BC. This 483 years ended when Jesus died upon the cross.

The period of time from the death of Jesus until the Rapture of the Church is called the Church Age. This period of time is parenthetical to the normal flow of the prophecy of the *"Seventy weeks."* The Church was not a part of the first 69 weeks, or 483 years, and it **will not** be a part of the final week, or seven years of the Tribulation period. Jesus said, *"Since you have kept my command to endure patiently, I will also keep you from the hour of trial that is going to come upon the whole world to test those who live on the earth."* (Rev. 3:10 NIV) The Church will not be on the earth to endure the trials of the Tribulation.

It is possible that the Church will still be on the earth during the time of the coming of Antichrist. In Dan. 9:27, we are told that Antichrist will *"confirm the covenant with many for one week."* The first thing we need to know is who is this *"many"* that a covenant is made with? We must look at the prophecy to get this answer. In Dan. 9:24, we are told that *"Seventy weeks are determined upon thy people and upon thy holy city...,"* which has been previously stated that this is the Jews and Jerusalem. We must remember that this prophecy is to the people of Israel. Therefore, the *"covenant"* must be with Israel. Antichrist will make a *"covenant"* or peace agreement with Israel for a period of seven years, or *"one week."* But in order for him to do so, he must be in a position politically and powerful enough militarily. It was briefly mentioned earlier that it is possible that a war could bring about the reformation of the ten kingdoms within the Old Roman Empire. These ten kingdoms **will** exist no matter how they come into being. Antichrist will be the king or ruler over one of these ten kingdoms. Therefore, I submit that as a king over one of these ten kingdoms within the Revised Roman Empire, he will have the power both politically and militarily to make this *"covenant"* with Israel.

Nothing in the Bible is said where the Church will be at the time this *"covenant"* with Israel is made. It could already be *"caught up"* before the agreement is made, or it could still be on the earth at that time. At any rate, whether the Church is still on the earth or not, it will be *"caught up"* once this *"covenant"* is made with Israel.

The making of this *"covenant"* with Israel marks the beginning of the Seventieth week, or the Tribulation period. Therefore, if the Church was not a part of the first 69 weeks, or 483 years of the prophecy of the *"Seventy weeks,"* it **will not** be a part of the final seven years of the prophecy. It is very possible that the Church will be taken out of the earth at the time that the *"covenant"* is made with Israel. I am not trying to set any particular date as to when the Church will be *"caught up."* But we **can** know the season and by reading the Bible, we **can** determine that the Church **cannot** be a part of the prophecy of the *"Seventy weeks."*

Why would this king of one of the ten kingdoms of the Revised Roman Empire make a *"covenant"* with Israel? It is clear from many scriptures in the Bible that Israel's temple will be rebuilt and they will again offer sacrifices and worship in this temple. (See Dan. 9:27; St. Matt 24:15; 2 Thess. 2:3-4; Rev. 11:1-2; 13:1-18) It is not clear, however, when the temple will be rebuilt. It could be completed before the Rapture of the Church or afterwards. In either case, it **will** be rebuilt and it **will** be completed before the middle of the final seven years of the prophecy of the *"Seventy weeks."* It is very probable that during the time of the rebuilding of the temple, the Jews will begin the sacrifices and worshipping. It could be that the Apostate Church, which will be headed up by the *"false prophet,"* (Rev. 13:11-17; 19:20; 20:10) will be persecuting the Jews while they are rebuilding their temple. It is very probable that Antichrist will make the *"covenant"* with Israel, promising to protect them while they complete the rebuilding of the temple and allow them to offer their sacrifices and worship freely.

A. Prophecies of the Tribulation Period

"Seventy weeks are determined upon thy people and upon thy holy city, to finish the transgression, and to make an end of sins, and to make reconciliation for iniquity, and to bring in everlasting righteousness, and to seal up the vision and prophecy, and to anoint the most Holy." (Dan. 9:24)

"And he shall confirm the covenant with many for one week;..." (Dan. 9:27)

"Watch out that no one deceives you. For many will come in my name, claiming, 'I am the Christ,' and will deceive many. You will hear of wars and rumors of wars, but see to it that you are not alarmed. Such things must happen, but the end is still to come.

Nation will rise against nation, and kingdom against kingdom. There will be famines and earthquakes in various places. All these are the beginning of birth pains....So when you see standing in the holy place the abomination that causes desolation, spoken of through the prophet Daniel—let the reader understand—then let those who are in Judea flee to the mountains....For then there will be great distress, unequaled from the beginning of the world until now—and never to be equaled again." (St. Matt. 24: 4-21 NIV) (See also St. Matt. 24:22-35)

"Because thou hast kept the word of my patience, I also will keep thee from the hour of temptation, which shall come upon all the world, to try them that dwell upon the earth." (Rev. 3:10)

The above scriptures are only a few of the prophecies of the Tribulation period. The fact that the Tribulation period will come **is** true. There are some that believe that we are now living in the Tribulation period. This cannot be so. Although we do seem to have a lot of wars and there are seemingly always rumors of wars, this does not mean the Tribulation period is now ongoing. There have been a lot of earthquakes and more seemingly every year. The weather patterns seem to be different than in years past. Volcanoes seem to be more active than ever before. Violence has increased in recent years. But, as long as the Church is on the earth, the Church Age is **still** ongoing and the Tribulation period is **yet** future.

The Tribulation period will begin as soon as the *"covenant"* is made with Israel, and the Church is *"caught up"* to be with Jesus. The events of Revelation portray the Tribulation period, and from chapter 4:1 and onward, the last half of the Tribulation period is the main course, with the exception of some parenthetical events interjected at times. When studying Revelation, one must keep in mind that although it is written mostly in chronological order, there are certain events that are parenthetical to normal flow of the book.

B. The Seventieth Week

"And here is the mind which hath wisdom. The seven heads are seven mountains, on which the woman sitteth. And there are seven kings: five are fallen, and one is. And the other is not yet come; and when he cometh, he must continue a short space. And the beast that was, and is not, even he is the eighth, and goeth into perdition. And the ten horns which thou sawest are ten kings, who have received no kingdom as yet, but receive power as kings one hour with the beast. These have one mind, and shall give their power and strength unto the beast." (Rev. 17:9-13)

In these verses of scripture we are told that *the "seven heads"* are *"seven kings."* We are told that *"five are fallen."* These five kings are the kings of the empires that had once ruled. They are Egypt, Assyria, Babylon, Medo-Persia and Greece. These five *"are fallen,"* meaning they no longer exist. We are told that *"one is."* At the time of this prophecy, the empire in power was the Roman Empire, which is the sixth empire. (The old Roman Empire ended in AD 476.) We are told that there will be another empire but it has *"not yet come."* This next empire that is yet to come **will be** the Revised Roman Empire. It will be made up of ten kingdoms and we are told that they will *"receive power as kings one hour with the beast."* The fact that it says they will serve as kings *"one hour"* means they will only reign as kings for a short period of time. But we are told that *"the beast that was, and is not, even he is the eighth, and goeth into perdition."* (vs.11) This eighth king or kingdom will be the Revived Grecian Empire, over which Antichrist will be King. He is the *"man of sin—the son of perdition"* (2 Thess.2:3) and he *"goeth into perdition."* (Rev. 17:11) Antichrist will fight a war with three of the ten kingdoms within the Revised Roman Empire, and he will *"subdue"* them. (Dan. 7:24) Then news of countries out of the east and north mounting an aggression against the Revived Grecian Empire (Dan. 11:44) causes the remaining six kings within the Revised Roman Empire to *"give their power and strength"* (Rev. 17:13) to Antichrist in order to fight against these warring countries. Therefore, Antichrist will then have control over the Revised Roman Empire as well as the Revived Grecian Empire.

1. The First Half of the Week—3 ½ Years

The establishing of a *"covenant"* with Israel by Antichrist marks the beginning of the Seventieth Week. (Dan. 9:27) Antichrist will then become involved with a war, which will be ongoing for the first half of the Tribulation period. We are told, *"At the time of the end the king of the South will engage him in battle, and the king of the North will storm out against him with chariots and cavalry and a great fleet of ships. He will invade many countries and sweep through them like a flood."* (Dan. 11:40 NIV) This war will be between the *"king of the South,"* which is Egypt, and the *"king of the North,"* which is Antichrist, who is the king of Syria. We know this because Syria borders Israel on the north and Egypt borders Israel on the south. (It must be kept in mind that Israel is the central focus of the prophecy.) We are told that Antichrist will *"storm out against"* the *"king of the South."* He will fight with great fury and he will *"subdue three kings."* (Dan. 7:24) The *"three kings"* that he is able to *"subdue"* are Egypt, Greece and Turkey. Once he gains victory over these three kings, he will have succeeded in bringing the old Grecian Empire back into one group. These four kingdoms, i.e. Egypt, Greece, Turkey and Syria, become the Revived Grecian Empire. It will take the entire first half, 3 ½ years, of the Tribulation period for Antichrist to *"subdue"* these three kingdoms and gain control over the entire Revised Roman Empire.

The Revived Grecian Empire will be made up of the kingdoms of Egypt, Greece, Turkey and Syria. Once these kingdoms become the Revived Grecian Empire under the rule of Antichrist, the remaining six kingdoms of the Revised Roman Empire will give their power and authority to Antichrist. (Rev. 17:13) As stated earlier, the reason these six kings of the Revised Roman Empire give their authority and power to Antichrist is that the news of war with countries out of the east and north causes them to want to ally themselves with Antichrist to be able to win this war. This will give Antichrist power over the entire Revised Roman Empire, which includes the Revived Grecian Empire.

The understanding that Antichrist will rule the world is a misconception. He will be a world ruler, in the same way as the President of the United States is considered a world ruler. However, Antichrist will not rule the entire world. He will rule over only those areas that he has authority over, which are the kingdoms within the Revised Roman Empire. Many countries outside the Revised Roman Empire will not come under the authority of Antichrist.

2. The Middle of the Week

"…and in the midst of the week he shall cause the sacrifice and the oblation to cease, and for the overspreading of abominations he shall make it desolate,…" (Dan. 9:27)

At the end of the first three and one half years of the Tribulation period, Antichrist will have succeeded in gaining control over all of the Revised Roman Empire, which includes all of the Revived Grecian Empire. Once this is done, Antichrist will then break the *"covenant"* that he has made with Israel. He will seek to destroy all of Jerusalem and those who do not bow down to his authority. We are told that he will enter the temple of the Jews and *"shall cause the sacrifice and oblation to cease."* He will demand that he be worshipped as God. He will demand that all people within his kingdom and Israel receive a mark attesting to their devotion to him. Those who do not receive this *"mark"* will be hunted and many will be murdered.

There will be many who will escape and survive the horrors of the *"man of sin."* (2 Thess. 2:3) *"So when you see standing in the holy place the abomination that causes desolation, spoken of through the prophet Daniel—let the reader understand— then let those who are in Judea flee to the mountains."* (St. Matt. 24:15-16 NIV) We are told that those in Judea should flee to the mountains when Antichrist enters into the temple and desolates it.

"And the woman fled into the wilderness, where she hath a place prepared by God, that they should feed her there a thousand two hundred and threescore days." (Rev. 12:6)

"And to the woman were given two wings of a great eagle, that she might fly into the wilderness, into her place, where she is nourished for a time, and times, and half a time, from the face of the serpent." (Rev. 12:14)

The fact that we are told that the *"woman"* is *"given two wings of a great eagle, that she might fly into the wilderness,"* is suggestive that this is a hasty flight away from Israel and the *"man of sin."* They are to leave everything behind and get out very quickly. (St. Matt. 24:16-20)

Where is this place in *"the wilderness"* or the *"mountains"* that these verses refer to? It is a place once called Petra, or Sela. It is a place in Edom, or Jordan, that is very mountainous and extremely rugged. It is about one hundred miles long and about a half mile wide in places. It will be in Jordan that the *"woman,"* or the remnants of Israel, will be cared for and looked after. Here Israel will be protected and Antichrist will not find them.

Antichrist will chase after those who flee, but God will intervene and protect them in their escape. Antichrist would probably continue his pursuit if possible, but he receives news of imminent war with the countries that are to the east and north. (Dan. 11:44) He is then preoccupied with this war which will last for most of the final half of the Tribulation period. We are told that the *"woman,"* who are the remnants of Israel, who flee to Jordan, will be fed and housed there for a period of time said to be *"a thousand two hundred and threescore days,"* or *"a time, and times, and half a time."* These two periods of time mentioned here are the same. The 1260 days are the same as the *"time, and times, and half a time."* Both are a total of three and a half- (3 ½) years. This will be the last half of the Tribulation period.

3. The Last Half of the Week—3 ½ Years

As already mentioned, Antichrist will become occupied with a war that will last most all of the last half of the final week of Daniel's prophecy of the *"Seventy weeks."* During this last half of the *"week,"* the trials that are to come upon the earth will escalate. (These trials will be discussed in the next chapter.) Also, the war that occupies Antichrist will be ongoing. This war will be between Antichrist, who is the Ruler over the Revised Roman Empire, which includes the Revived Grecian Empire, and the countries *"out of the east and out of the north."* (Dan. 11:45 See also Ezek. 38-39) Who are these countries that war against Antichrist? It is my belief that they are Russia, who is the country north of the Revised Roman Empire, and the oriental countries, i.e. China, Cambodia, Taiwan, Laos, Viet Nam, etc., east of the Revised Roman Empire. Other countries of Asian and Arab culture may also be involved. Antichrist will win this war eventually, but it takes most of the last half of the Tribulation period, or the last half of the final *"week"* of the seventieth week, to do so.

Once this war is ended, Antichrist will then again turn his attention to Israel. He will again come against Israel to destroy those who he believes are in rebellion against him and who have not yet taken the *"mark."* His intention is also to wage war against Jesus to prevent Him from setting up His earthly kingdom. Antichrist will order his armies, who are the armies of those defeated by him in all the previous wars and those who decide to ally themselves with him, to gather at a place called *"Armageddon."* (Rev. 16:16) (This event will be discussed in the next chapter.) It will be during this war that Antichrist and his followers will meet disaster. Jesus will defeat them and they will no longer exist once this battle is finished.

Chapter Six
EVENTS OF THE TRIBULATION PERIOD

Many events will take place during the Tribulation period other than those already mentioned. Some of the events that have been already briefly mentioned will be discussed in more detail, as well as others. The Tribulation period will be a time of trial that will come upon the entire world. However, most of the trials will be upon those within the Revised Roman Empire, of which Israel is part. It must be kept in mind that the events that are to take place during the Tribulation period are interjected with parenthetical events that do not disrupt the normal flow of events, but rather, they help to add better understanding to what is going on during the time. These parenthetical events will be discussed a little later in this chapter.

1. The Seven-Sealed Book

"And I saw lying on the open hand of Him Who was seated on the throne a (book) scroll written within and on the back, closed and sealed with seven seals; And I saw a strong angel announcing in a loud voice, Who is worthy to open the scroll? And—who is entitled and deserves and is morally fit—to break the seals?...See, the Lion of the tribe of Judah, the Root (Source) of David, has won—has overcome and conquered! He can open the scroll and break its seven seals!" (Rev. 5:1,2,5 Amp. Bible)

The scene here is in Heaven, and we are told that a book or scroll *"written within and on the back"* was presented. It was *"closed and sealed with seven seals."* In the following verses we see that a search was made for one that is worthy to open the book and break the seals. Then in verse 5 we are told that the *"Lion of Judah, the Root (Source) of David...He can open the scroll and break its seven seals."* This *"Lion of Judah"* is Jesus and He has *"overcome and conquered"* the enemy, who is Satan, and it is He Who can open the scroll and break its seals.

As each of the seals is broken, and the contents read, there are different trials that come forth. As we read Revelation, we notice that the opening of the seals are in a chronological order. When the seventh seal is opened, another series of seven judgments come forth called the trumpet judgments. Then out of the seventh trumpet come forth seven vials, or bowl judgments. However, all of the trumpet and bowl judgments are contained in the seventh seal. Therefore, the seven seals actually make up the whole of these judgments.

a. The First Seal: False Christ

"Then I saw as the Lamb broke open one of the seven seals, and as if in a voice of thunder I heard one of the four living creatures call out, Come! And I looked, and saw there a white horse whose rider carried a bow. And a crown was given him, and he rode forth conquering and to conquer." (Rev. 6:1,2 Amp. Bible)

The *"four living creatures"* in this verse are spoken of in more detail in Rev. 4:6-11. They continually *"give glory and honor and thanks to him that is seated on the throne, who liveth forever and ever."* (Rev. 4:9) One of these creatures speaks and we are told that his voice was *"as if in a voice of thunder."* He says to the writer, *"Come."*

The *"Lamb"* is the same as the *"Lion of Judah."* He is Jesus, Who, as mentioned above, is the One worthy to *"open the scroll and break its seals.* " When He does so, we are told that John, the writer of Revelation, sees a *"white horse"* and the one riding it had a *"bow; and a crown was given unto him, and he went forth conquering, and to conquer."* Who is this rider of a white horse? He is the *"man of sin,"* (2 Thess. 2:3) the *"beast"* of Rev. 13:1 and the *"little horn"* of Dan. 7:8. This person is Antichrist who will be given authority as King over all of the Revised Roman Empire. (Rev. 17:13)

When the Revised Roman Empire comes into existence it will be comprised of ten kingdoms with each ruled by its own king. Antichrist will be one of the kings over one of these kingdoms. To be exact, he will be the king of the Syrian kingdom, which includes Iran, Iraq and parts of Saudi Arabia. Antichrist, as stated earlier, will make a *"covenant"*, or peace agreement, with Israel for a period of seven years. This will mark the beginning of the final week of the *"Seventy weeks"* prophecy.

During the first half of this final week, Antichrist will be engaged in a war with three of the ten kingdoms within the Revised Roman Empire. He will win this war and by doing so, he will have succeeded in regrouping the old Grecian Empire, which is called the Revived Grecian Empire. He will then enter into Jerusalem, and go into the temple that the Jews have finished rebuilding, and he will set himself up as God and demand that all people worship him as God. He will break the *"covenant"* he had made with Israel, and cause the Jewish sacrifices and worshipping to cease. (Dan. 9:27) He and the *"false prophet"* persecute those who do not submit to his authority and cause many to receive a *"mark"* to identify them as his followers. (Rev. 13:11-18) He then receives news *"out of the east and out of the north"* of imminent war and *"he shall go forth with great fury to destroy, and utterly sweep away."* (Dan. 11:44) The kings of the remaining six kingdoms within the Revised Roman Empire will then give their power and authority to Antichrist and together they will win this war.

This war will continue for most of the final half of the Tribulation period. Antichrist will then turn his attention again to Jerusalem and bring all the armies under his command and those who will ally with him to destroy the Jews. This is his pretense; however, he will have a larger plan in mind. He will seek to wage war against Jesus, Who comes to earth to establish His earthly kingdom. Therefore, as seen here, Antichrist will come into power *"conquering, and to conquer."*

b. The Second Seal: War

"And when He broke the second seal, I heard the second living creature call out, Come! And another horse came out, flaming red. And its rider was empowered to take peace from the earth, so that men slaughtered one another; and he was given a huge sword." (Rev. 6:3,4 Amp. Bible)

The second seal is opened and we are told that a horse that is *"flaming red"* comes forth. The rider on this horse has the power given to him to *"take peace from the earth."* As stated above, when Antichrist comes on the scene, he will come *"conquering, and to conquer."* He will be engaged in war for most all of the Tribulation period. His first war will be with Egypt, who is *"the king of the south."* (Dan. 11:40) In this war, Turkey and Greece will ally themselves with Egypt and they will be defeated by the *"king of the north,"* (Dan. 11:40) who is Antichrist, the king of the Syrian Kingdom. This will establish the Revived Grecian Empire. This first war will last for three and one half years, the first half of the Tribulation period.

The second war that Antichrist will be engaged in will be with the countries *"out of the east and out of the north."* (Dan. 11:44 See also Ezek. 38-39) When he receives news of this imminent war, the kings of the remaining six kingdoms within the Revised Roman Empire give their power and authority to him, and they engage in war. (Rev. 17:13) This war will last for most of the last half of the Tribulation period. Antichrist will then turn his attention to Jerusalem once again to destroy the Jews. However, as stated above, he has a much bigger plan in mind, that of waging war against the Son of God, Jesus, when He comes to establish His earthly kingdom. Antichrist dares to believe that he can prevent Jesus from succeeding in setting up His kingdom on earth. It will be in this battle that Antichrist will meet with disaster.

From the beginning of the Tribulation period, to the end of it, there will be war. Therefore, when the second seal is opened, the rider of the red horse does take peace from the earth and men will slaughter one another.

c. The Third Seal: Famine

"When He broke open the third seal, I heard the third living creature call out, Come and look! And I saw, and behold, a black horse, and in his hand the rider had a pair of scales (a balance). And I heard what seemed to be a voice from the midst of the four living creatures saying, a quart of wheat for a denarius (a whole day's wages), and three quarts of barley for a denarius; but do not harm the oil and the wine!" (Rev. 6:5,6 Amp. Bible)

When Jesus opens the third seal, John sees a *"black horse"* come forth and its rider has in his hand *"a scale"* or balance. We are told that *"a quart of wheat for a denarius (a whole day's wages), and three quarts of barley for a denarius; but do not harm the oil and the wine!"* This is representative of famine. Anytime there is war, there always follows famine. Because of the huge costs of financing war, the destruction of property, and shortages of food, the necessities of life become scarce. The prices that is depicted for someone to buy *"a quart of wheat"* for a *"whole day's wages"* is indicative that for a family of three, it would take all the money a man would make to feed his family for one day. Food, in the aftermath of war, is usually scarce, whereas other less needed supplies such as oil and wine would be in ample surplus. If you have plenty of oil with which to cook, and wine to drink, what good is that when there is no food with which to cook with the oil? The oil and the wine do not sustain life. Therefore, in many cases, starvation seems to be the result of famine.

d. The Fourth Seal: Death

"When the Lamb broke open the fourth seal, I heard the fourth living creature call out, Come! So I looked, and behold, an ashy pale horse (black and blue as if made so by bruising), and its rider's name was Death, and Hades (the realm of the dead) followed him closely; and they were given authority and power over a fourth part of the earth, to kill with the sword and with famine and with plague (pestilence, disease) and with wild beasts of the earth." (Rev. 6:7, 8 Amp. Bible)

The fourth seal is opened and there comes forth *"an ashy pale horse."* We are told that the *"rider's name was Death, and Hades (the realm of the dead) followed him closely."* These were *"given authority and power over a fourth of the earth, to kill with the sword and with famine and with plague (pestilence, disease) and with wild beasts of the earth."* The previous seal contained famine. Death follows famine in most cases. But as if the famine of the third seal was not enough, now the famine gets worse and spreads to include a fourth part of the earth. People will be so desperate that they will kill others for whatever food they can get. Even the wild beasts of the earth will be effected and they too will search out people to be able to satisfy their hunger. All this will bring about plague and disease. This will be a time of unprecedented trouble such as was never known. The trials that come upon the earth during the Tribulation period will be horrifying! For those who must live through this period of time, it will be a time of great fear. But those who become followers of Christ will know that they have comfort in Him. Many will suffer during this time, however, those who trust in Jesus will be ready when they are to give up their lives for the Lord. This will indeed be a time of great tribulation for those who will have to endure this trial.

e. The Fifth Seal: The Martyred Remnant

"When the Lamb broke open the fifth seal, I saw at the foot of the altar the souls of those whose lives had been sacrificed for (adhering to) the Word of God and for the testimony they had borne. They cried in a loud voice, O (Sovereign) Lord, holy and true, how long now before You will sit in judgment and avenge our blood upon those who dwell on the earth? Then they were each given a long and flowing and festive white robe and told to rest and wait patiently a little while longer, until the number should be complete of their fellow servants and their brethren, who were to be killed as they themselves had been." (Rev. 6:9-11 Amp. Bible)

When the fifth seal is opened, the scene changes from earth to heaven. John now sees a vision of those that will be killed, or martyred, for their faith in God. These who are martyred cry out to God, *"how long now before You will sit in judgment and avenge our blood upon those who dwell on the earth?"* It is significant that these who are slain because of their faith are asking God when He will avenge their blood on those who still living on the earth. Therefore, these were slain during the time of the Tribulation period. The saints of God of the Church Age have already been *"caught up"* to be with Jesus. It cannot be these or any others prior to the Rapture, as some suggest. It **must** be the saints who have been killed for their faith in Christ during the Tribulation period.

The fact that the martyrs ask for judgment upon those that dwell on the earth is suggestive that those that had persecuted them are yet living. However, they are told that they must *"wait patiently a little while longer, until the number should be complete of their fellow servants and their brethren, who were to be killed as they themselves had been."* Thus, it is evident that others are to be killed for their faith and their testimony. It makes it clear now that in the time of the Tribulation period it will be difficult to mention to others openly about the faith they have in God. In doing so could seriously jeopardize their lives. But one must not conceal the fact that they are followers of Christ, for in doing so, you risk losing your salvation. By admitting and witnessing your faith in God to others, you will risk death. And many will die, as seen in this vision.

The martyrs are *"each given a long and flowing and festive white robe."* The fact that these are not yet resurrected, and will not be resurrected until the end of the Tribulation period, is proof that they are those who will die for their faith and testimony during the Tribulation period. They are not the saints of the Church Age, nor are they the Old Testament saints. Since they are not yet resurrected, the question is, what kind of body do these martyrs have, if they are given robes? They will be given a temporary body, different from that of the glorified body of the Church Age saints. This temporary body will not be their resurrected body, but will be a body suitable for their presence in Heaven. These will, however, be replaced by their resurrected bodies at the time of their resurrection at the close of the Tribulation period.

Some who study Revelation say that because these who are martyred and are told to *"wait patiently a little while longer,"* proves that they were killed during the first half of the Tribulation period, and that others will be killed during the last half of the period. In studying Revelation, we find that at no place does it speak of a total of seven years. Revelation speaks only of forty-two months, three and a half years, or a similar designation. Therefore, Revelation speaks only of the last half of the seven-year period. But, the first three seals take in the first part of the Tribulation, whereas Antichrist is introduced and he comes peacefully at first, but bringing in war soon afterwards. However, the contents of the fourth and fifth seals are in the final half of the Tribulation period. In trying not to confuse anyone, it must be said that most of Revelation deals with only the final three and a half years of the Seventieth week. But it does refer back to the first half from time to time, such as the rise of Antichrist in chapter thirteen and the greatness of Babylon in chapter seventeen and others.

f. The Sixth Seal: Anarchy

"When He (the Lamb) broke open the sixth seal, I looked, and there was a great earthquake; and the sun grew black as sackcloth of hair, (the full disc of) the moon became like blood. And the stars of the sky dropped to the earth like a fig tree shedding its unripe fruit out of season when shaken by a strong wind. And the sky rolled up like a scroll and vanished, and every mountain and island was dislodged from its place. Then the kings of the earth and their noblemen and their magnates and their military chiefs and the wealthy and the strong and (everyone, whether) slave or free, hid themselves in the caves and among the rocks of the mountains, And they called to the mountains and the rocks, Fall on (before) us and hide us from the face of Him Who sits on the throne, and from the deep seated indignation and wrath of the Lamb. For the great day of His wrath (vengeance, retribution, indignation) has come, and who is able to stand before it?" (Rev. 6:12-17 Amp. Bible)

As soon as the sixth seal is opened, John says there was a *"great earthquake."* He then goes on to tell about the sun becoming blackened and the stars falling from the heavens like *"a fig tree shedding its unripe fruit out of season when shaken by a strong wind."* He says that the *"sky rolled up like a scroll and vanished, and every mountain and island was dislodged from its place.*" Some believe that all this is symbolic and that it will not literally happen. However, at the time of God's intervening with the blasphemous and wickedness of mankind, it would seem that this would be a literal shaking of the elements. The people of the earth at this time will realize that the *"great day of His (God's) wrath has come."* We are told that they will call out to the mountains and the rocks to *"Fall on us."* They are afraid of the vengeance that is about to take place, and they desire to be hid *"from the face of Him Who sits on the throne, and from the deep seated indignation and wrath of the Lamb."* They ask, *"who is able to stand before it?"* They know that they have been wicked and they cannot bare to look upon the face of Jesus and see His wrath.

The opening of the sixth seal is the beginning of the severe trials that will come upon mankind on the earth. Since this is only the sixth seal, and there yet comes the seventh in which there will be seven trumpet judgments and then seven bowl judgments, this only marks the beginning of the severity of the trials to come. To understand this prophecy to be symbolic would be a mistake in that, if it were, no one would really feel the fear that the people of the earth will literally feel. Yet they will not repent and turn to God. Instead they will curse Him and continue in their vile and wicked ways.

g. Interlude Between the Sixth and Seventh Seal

The events of Revelation 7 are parenthetical to the normal flow of the opening of the seals. These events do not advance the narrative but directs our attention to two major groups of saints during the time of the Tribulation period. This chapter speaks of the Jews and Gentiles that will be saved during the Tribulation. It also speaks of the Remnant of one hundred forty four thousand out of Israel and the great multitude who come out of the great Tribulation. This parenthetical chapter will be discussed a little later, as well as others.

h. The Seventh Seal

"When He (the Lamb) broke open the seventh seal, there was silence for about half an hour in heaven. Then I saw the seven angels who stand before God, and to them were given seven trumpets. And another angel came and stood over the altar. He had a golden censer, and he was given very much incense (fragrant spices and gums which exhale perfume when burned), that he might mingle it with the prayers of all the people of God (the saints) upon the altar of gold before the throne. And the smoke of the incense (the perfume) arose in the presence of God with the prayers of the people of God (the saints) from the hand of the angel. So the angel took the censer and filled it with fire from the altar and cast it upon the earth. Then there followed thunder peals and loud rumblings and blasts and noises, and lightning flashes, and an earthquake. Then the seven angels who had the seven trumpets prepared to sound them." (Rev. 8:1-6 Amp. Bible)

When the seventh seal is opened, we are told that *"there was silence for about half an hour in heaven."* Nothing is said to explain this silence for half an hour. However, I submit that perhaps it could be silent for this period of time to hear the cries, or prayers for deliverance from the sufferings of the Christians on earth. Furthermore, this silence may be in anticipation of what is about to happen in the following judgments that will be pronounced upon the earth and those that dwell therein. Half of an hour is not a long period of time, however, it is seemingly a long period of time when one is eagerly awaiting something or some news that may be of great importance to someone.

John then sees seven angels who are *"given seven trumpets."* These seven angels prepare to *"sound"* the trumpets, but before doing so, *"another angel came and stood over the altar."* It has been argued as to who this angel is. Some say that he is an angel of high rank who is designated to perform certain duties before God. Others claim this angel to be an angelic representation of the Lord Jesus Christ. Although we are not told specifically who this angel is, it would seem that since he is given a *"censer"* and other items with which he can perform certain duties in much the same order as a high priest, then the latter of these two opinions seems more preferred.

We are not told the meaning of what the *"incense"* is. That it is mingled with *"the prayers of all the people of God,"* which are the saints on earth at the time, suggests it brings about an aroma pleasing unto God, and He is about to answer the prayers He hears. The *"smoke of the incense"* rises *"in the presence of God"* and the angel casts it *"upon the earth."* We are told that *"there followed thunder peals and loud rumblings and blasts and noises, and lightning flashes, and an earthquake."* This apparently is an announcement of the soon to follow judgments that are about to come forth from the trumpets as the angels sound them in succession. It announces the impending trials and hardships that will come upon the earth and those that dwell therein. These judgments will be upon those who deny God and who curse and blaspheme His name. Once the *"incense"* is cast upon the earth, now the angels prepare to sound each of the trumpets.

1. The First Trumpet Judgment

"The first angel blew (his) trumpet, and there was a storm of hail and fire mingled with blood, cast upon the earth. And a third part of the earth was burned up, and a third part of the trees was burned up and all the green grass was burned up." (Rev. 8:7 Amp. Bible)

Many teachers of Revelation try to state that some of the judgments in the book are symbolic and that they have no literal meaning. There is no reason for not accepting these judgments as literal. The Great Tribulation period, which is the last half of the *"Seventieth week,"* will be a time of horrific trials and judgments. Mankind has degraded himself to that of mostly demon-like behavior without any regard for God. Therefore, I submit that the judgments within Revelation are not only literal in meaning, but also justified by God.

In this verse we see that a *"third part of the earth was burned up"* and a third of all the trees and *"all the green grass"* was burned up. This judgment is a judgment against the vegetation on earth. The fact that we are told that *"blood"* is mingled with the hail and the fire seems to indicate that those who are caught in the *"storm"* would be slain. Whether there will actually be blood mixed with the fire and hail, or if it is the result of the shedding of the blood of mankind if caught in the storm is not really an issue. The results will be the same.

This judgment, terrible as it is, marks only the beginning of greater judgments yet to come. There are six more trumpet judgments that follow this one, and each one is more severe. The seventh trumpet will open to seven more judgments, the bowl judgments, which will be greater than those previous. Therefore, it will be a time of *"weeping and gnashing of teeth."* (St. Matt. 24:51)

2. The Second Trumpet Judgment

"The second angel blew his trumpet, and something resembling a great mountain, blazing with fire, was hurled into the sea. And a third of the sea was turned to blood. A third of the living creatures in the sea perished, an a third of the ships were destroyed." (Rev. 8:8,9 Amp. Bible)

When the second angel blows the trumpet, John sees *"something resembling a great mountain, blazing with fire"* being cast into the sea. The King James Version says that it was a *"mountain."* I cannot believe this to be symbolic in any way. As stated earlier, these judgments **must** be interpreted as literal where it is possible to do so. The fact that it looks like or resembles a *"mountain"* and that it is said to be *"blazing with fire,"* it is evident that John is seeing a huge asteroid falling from the heavens and smashing into the sea. We have known of many asteroids falling from space in the past. Some have been large enough to create large craters in the earth. What John sees here is most likely a very large asteroid. When an asteroid, or meteor enters into earth's atmosphere, the friction and speed would cause it to become a *"blazing"* asteroid. I believe this is exactly what John sees in this vision.

We are told that this *"mountain"* is *"hurled into the sea."* A third of all *"living creatures"* in the sea where this impact would be will be killed. Any ships in that area would also be totally destroyed and the lives of persons aboard those ships would be lost. This judgment is upon the sea, just as the previous judgment was upon the vegetation on earth. A third of the sea on earth is turned to blood, thus the destruction of marine life and the lives of mankind who are aboard the ships at the time this *"mountain"* impacts the sea. This will be a literal judgment that will literally destroy a third of the sea and a third of marine life and ships in the sea. To believe it to be non-literal would be to disbelieve God's Word.

3. The Third Trumpet Judgment

"The third angel blew (his) trumpet, and a huge star fell from heaven, burning like a torch. And it dropped on a third of the rivers and on the springs of water. And the name of the star is Wormwood. A third part of the waters was changed into wormwood, and many people died from using the water, because it had become bitter." (Rev. 8:10,11 Amp. Bible)

Here, again, John sees something falling from the heavens. He says that it is a *"huge star...burning like a torch."* There have been some teachers who have tried to say that this judgment is symbolic and assigned it to the fall of Satan from heaven into the earth. In the symbolic view, Satan is the *"star...burning like a torch"* and his name is here called *"Wormwood."* The *"rivers"* and the *"springs of water,"* in this view, are representative of the people who dwell upon the earth. This cannot be the proper interpretation . It is preferable to view this judgment, as with the others, to be literal, and that it is actually a *"star"* or asteroid, or meteor that falls from the heavens and drops *"on a third of the rivers and on the springs of water."* One might ask how this can be, seeing that a third of the rivers and the springs of water of the earth are not all gathered into one place. It is possible that after the *"star"* enters earth's atmosphere, it could be broken into several pieces, thereby falling on a third of the rivers and springs of water. Although it is not said how this will be done, it must be understood that it will be done!

The *"star"* is named *"Wormwood."* We are told that when the *"star"* drops into a third of the rivers and springs of water, a *"third part of the waters was changed to wormwood, and many died from using the water, because it had become bitter."* When this event occurs, it is possible that the meteor will have a chemical effect on the waters and perhaps poison the waters. People who use this poisoned water will die from the poison or chemical changes of the water. It is evident here that this judgment is upon mankind.

4. The Fourth Trumpet Judgment

"Then the fourth angel blew (his) trumpet, and a third of the sun was smitten, and a third of the moon, and a third of the stars, so that (the light of) a third of them was darkened, and a third of the daylight (itself) was withdrawn and likewise a third (of the light) of the night was kept from shining. Then I (looked and I) saw a solitary eagle flying in midheaven, and as it flew I heard it crying with a loud voice, Woe, woe, woe to those who dwell on the earth, because of the rest of the trumpet blasts which the three angels are about to sound!" (Rev.

8: 12, 13 Amp. Bible)

The first three trumpet judgments are upon the land, sea, rivers and fountains of water. Here the judgment is changed and is found to be upon the heavenly bodies. We are told that a third part of the sun, moon and stars are darkened so that they will not shine as brightly as before. This would extend to the light of the day and the night, whereas, if the sun, moon and stars were darkened, then it would mean the day and night would also be darkened somewhat. It would seem that this infers to the soon to come announcement of the next judgments that are yet to come.

In the King James Version of the Bible, verse 13 says *"And I beheld, and heard an angel flying through the midst of heaven...."* All the best manuscripts substitute *"eagle"* for *"angel."* Whether it is an angel or an eagle that is making the announcement is neither here nor there. The result is the same and the announcement is of the impending severity of the next three trumpet judgments. John sees and hears this angel, or eagle, as he announces *"Woe, woe, woe to those who dwell on the earth, because of the rest of the trumpet blasts which the three angels are about to sound."* The repetitious announcement of *"Woe, woe, woe"* signifies the greater severity of each trumpet judgment yet to come. Those on whom these woes are pronounced are *"those who dwell on the earth."* This is in reference to the wicked people still living and who have not become followers of Christ.

5. The Fifth Trumpet Judgment—First *"Woe"*

"Then the fifth angel blew (his) trumpet, and I saw a star that had fallen from the sky to the earth, and to the angel was given the key of the shaft of the abyss—the bottomless pit. He opened the long shaft of the abyss—the bottomless pit—and smoke like the smoke of a huge furnace puffed out of the long shaft, so that the sun and the

atmosphere were darkened by the smoke from the long shaft." (Rev. 9:1,2 Amp. Bible)

It is here in this trumpet judgment that the *"star"* is to be referred to as symbolic. This is not a literal star that falls from the heavens. This *"star"* is in direct reference to Satan. There is no mention as to the identity of this *"star,"* but the inference is the aftermath of the war in heaven where, as a result, Satan is cast into the earth. (See Rev. 12:7-12) We are told that *"to the angel was given the key of the shaft of the abyss — the bottomless pit."* Therefore, I submit that this *"angel"* is none other than Satan. He is the fallen angel, the angel who sinned in the beginning. (See Isa. 14:12-17)

In Rev 12:7-12, we have the account of the war in heaven. We are told, *"And there was war in heaven; Michael and his angels fought against the dragon, and the dragon fought and his angels, and prevailed not, neither was their place found any more in heaven. And the great dragon was cast out, that old serpent, called the Devil and Satan, who deceiveth the whole world; he was cast out into the earth, and his angels were cast out with him......Woe to the inhabiters of the earth and of the sea! For the devil is come down unto you, having great wrath, because he knoweth that he hath but a short time."* Therefore, this *"star"* is none other than Satan, and he brings in the first *"Woe"* to those who inhabit the earth.

We are told that to this *"star"*, or angel, is *"given the key of the shaft of the abyss — the bottomless pit."* The *"bottomless pit"* is the abode of the demons, according to Luke 8:31, where we are told that the demon that spoke to Jesus named *"Legion....because many (demons) were entered into him"* (St Luke 8:30) asked not to be sent *"into the deep."* In the cross reference, *"the deep"* is in reference to *"the bottomless pit."* This *"abyss"* is the place where the demons are held in detention, and Satan is given the key to open this abyss and release these demons. When Satan unlocks this abyss, we are told that *"smoke like the smoke of a huge furnace puffed out of the long shaft, so that the sun and the atmosphere were darkened by the smoke from the long shaft."* When this *"smoke"* erupts from the *"bottomless pit"* the sun and air are darkened, polluting the air and darkening the light of day. It is evident that the earth will be inundated by demonic and satanic influence. These demonic beings that will be loosed will torment the wicked and the wicked will still refuse to turn to God.

a. Demonic Torment of the Wicked

"Then out of the smoke locusts came forth on the earth, and such power was granted them as the power the earth's scorpions have. They were told not to injure the herbage of the earth nor any green thing nor any tree, but only (to attack) such human beings as do not have the seal (mark) of God on their foreheads. For they were not permitted to kill them, but to torment (distress, vex) them for five months, and the pain caused them was like the torture of a scorpion when it stings a person. And in those days people will seek death and will not find it, and they will yearn to die, but death evades and flees from them." (Rev. 9:3-6 Amp. Bible)

When Satan opens the *"bottomless pit,"* out of the smoke will come *"locusts"* upon the earth. We are told that these *"locusts"* will have the power to sting a person in the same manner as does the scorpion. They are commanded to not *"injure the herbage of the earth nor any green thing nor any tree."* They are *"to attack"* people who *"do not have the seal (mark) of God on their foreheads."* The people who do have the *"seal (mark) of God on their foreheads"* are those whom God seals with His mark to protect them during the Tribulation Period.

Earlier, I mentioned the interlude between the sixth and seventh seal judgments. During this interlude we are told that there were *"four angels stationed at the four corners of the earth, firmly holding back the four winds of the earth, so that no wind should blow on the earth or the sea or upon any tree."* Then John saw a *"second angel coming up from the east (the rising of the sun), and carrying the seal of the living God. And with a loud voice he called out to the four angels who had been given authority and power to injure the earth and sea, Saying, Harm neither the earth nor the sea nor the trees, until we have sealed the bond servants of our God upon their foreheads."* (Rev. 7:1-3 Amp. Bible) Then in the following verses we read about the 144,000 that are sealed. These 144,000 that are mentioned are sealed with the seal of God, as well as all those whom they minister to and are able to bring into the joys of serving God. Therefore, it is suggested that all who are, or become Christians during the Tribulation period will have the seal of God placed upon their foreheads. Whether this will be a visible seal is not known. More likely it will not be visible; rather it will be the knowledge of God in the minds of those who have turned their lives over to Him. God knows those who are His. Thus, the demon-like locusts will torment only those who do not have this seal of God in their foreheads. (The events of Rev. 7 will be discussed a little later in this chapter.)

We are told that the demon-like locusts are told not to harm any green thing or tree, but only to attack those who do not have the seal of God in their foreheads. The sting that they inflict on people will be like that of a scorpion sting. However, people will not die from this sting. The pain and torment will be so great that we are told that people will desire to die, but death will flee from them. We are told that this will continue for a period of five months. This is a literal five months and not symbolical. People will not be able to hide from these demons and they will be inflicted with torment for the entire five months. A scorpion sting is very painful. I was stung by a scorpion when I was in the jungles of Viet Nam in 1967/1968, and believe me, it is not a sting you soon forget. You **do not** want to be stung a second time! Those who do not have the seal of God in their foreheads, the wicked, will have to endure this pain and suffering for five long months! No wonder they will seek death. They will cry out in their pain for death to come, *"but death evades and flees from them."*

b. The Description of the Locusts

"The locusts resembled horses equipped for battle. On their heads was something like golden crowns. Their faces resembled the faces of people. They had hair like the hair of women, and their teeth were like lions' teeth. Their breastplates (scales) resembled breastplates made of iron, and the (whirring) noise made by their wings was like the roar of a vast number of horse-drawn chariots going at full speed into battle. They have tails like scorpions, and they have stings, and in their tails lies their ability to hurt men for (the) five months. Over them as king they have the angel of the abyss—of the bottomless pit. In Hebrew his name is Abaddon (destruction), but in Greek he is called Apollyon (destroyer)." (Rev. 9:7-11 Amp. Bible)

Here we have the description of these demons that inflict harm and pain upon wicked mankind. They are not like normal locusts and are not of the normal size of a locust or scorpion. We are told that they *"resemble horses equipped for battle."* Although demons normally do not have any shape or form, it is apparent that here they resemble horses. We are told that they have on their heads a *"crown"* which most likely is a headdress. Their *"breastplate (scales) resembled breastplates made of iron,"* which indicates the incapability to destroy them. We are told that their faces are like the faces of people and their hair like women's hair and teeth like that of the lions. This is picturesque of something utterly fearful and in keeping with the true nature of evil and Satan. These demonic creatures will have the power to *"hurt men for (the) five months"* that they are allowed to roam throughout the earth.

c. Two More Woes to Come

"The first woe (calamity) has passed; lo, two others are yet to follow." (Rev. 9:12 Amp. Bible)

As terrible as was the previous judgment with the locusts, this only marks the end of the first *"woe."* There are *"two others"* yet to follow. Each of the next trumpet judgments will be more severe than was the previous "woe." We are told in the Amplified Bible that the term *"woe"* means *"calamity."* In the previous judgment, men did not die, but the desire to die was great. Therefore, the calamity is not being able to rid them of the pain inflicted upon themselves either by death or by the destruction of the demons. Men will have to endure the pain and suffering for the entire five months and will not be able to escape.

6. The Sixth Trumpet Judgment—Second *"Woe"*

a. The Four Angels Loosed

"Then the sixth angel blew (his) trumpet, and from the four horns of the altar of gold which stands before God I heard a solitary voice, Saying to the sixth angel who had the trumpet, Liberate the four angels who are bound at the great river Euphrates. So the four angels, who had been in readiness for that hour in the appointed day, month and year, were liberated to destroy a third of mankind." (Rev. 9:13-15 Amp. Bible)

John hears the sixth angel blow his trumpet, which marks the beginning of the second *"woe."* When this trumpet is sounded, he hears a *"solitary voice"* speaking to the angel with the trumpet *"from the four horns of the altar of gold which stands before God."* This altar is the same altar as was in Rev. 8:3. However, the altar in 8:3 was where the offering of incense with the prayers of the saints was placed, whereas here, the altar is associated with the judgment of the sixth trumpet. It would seem that because this same altar is mentioned here, it is in reference to a response to the prayers of the saints and possibly an anticipation of readiness for their deliverance.

The *"voice"* says to *"Liberate the four angels, who are bound at the great river Euphrates."* These *"four angels"* are not identified, but it would seem that they are not holy angels, because of the statement that they have been *"bound"* at this river. No holy angel of God would be *"bound."* Therefore, this suggests that they are unholy angels. The fact that they are to be liberated, or set free, is indicative that they been held at the river Euphrates for a certain purpose.

In verse 15 we are told that the four angels that have been bound have been held here *"in readiness for that hour in the appointed day, month and year."* Therefore, it is evident that these unholy angels have an *"appointed"* mission to complete. That mission, as we are told, is to *"destroy a third of mankind."* In the previous judgments we were told that a *"fourth"* of mankind had been destroyed. Now another *"third"* are to be slain. When this judgment becomes fulfilled, over half of the earth's population will have been destroyed!

b. An Army of Two Hundred Million

"The number of their troops of cavalry was twice ten thousand times ten thousand (200,000,000); I heard what their number was. And in (my) vision the horses and their riders appeared to me like this: the riders wore breastplates the color of fiery red and sapphire blue and sulphur (brimstone) yellow. The heads of the horses looked like lion's heads, and from their mouths there poured fire and smoke and sulphur (brimstone). A third of mankind was killed by these three plagues, by the fire and the smoke and the sulphur (brimstone) that poured from the mouths of the horses. For the power of the horses to do harm is in their mouths and also in their tails. Their tails are

like serpents, for they have heads, and it is by means of them that they wound people." (Rev. 9:16-19 Amp. Bible)

John says the *"number of their troops of cavalry was twice ten thousand times ten thousand (200,000,000)."* This is a massive military force by any standard! Some believe that this number should not be taken as literal, rather it should only be considered as a very large and overwhelming force. They believe that this number represents an innumerable size military force that is beyond computation.

There is no statement as to the origin of this massive force. However, I remember that in the 1960's, China claimed to have a military force of over 200,000,000, which included both men and women. With the rapid growth of world population, that number very well could be half as much or more than that today! Therefore, it would seem that it could be possible to take this number to be literal. Literal or not, this **is** a massive army that is empowered to destroy a third of mankind.

John gives us an account of the description of this army. He said that he saw in his vision *"horses and their riders appeared to me like this: the riders wore breastplates the color of fiery red and sapphire blue and sulphur (brimstone) yellow. The heads of the horses looked like lion's heads, and from their mouths there poured fire and smoke and sulphur (brimstone)."* This description, it would seem, would be a symbolic picture of modern day mechanical warfare. In John's day, mechanical warfare was unheard of or even thought of. Therefore, it is possible that this is a picture of modern mechanical warfare in which a third of mankind would easily be slain. It is also possible that this scene coincides with the war that Antichrist will be engaged in with the countries *"out of the east and out of the north"* (Dan. 11:44) during the last half of the Tribulation period. It is very possible that during this war, a third of mankind would be destroyed.

c. Mankind Still Refuses To Repent

"And the rest of humanity, who were not killed by these plagues, even then did not repent (out) of (the worship of) the works of their (own) hands, so as to cease paying homage to the demons and idols of gold and silver and bronze and stone and wood, which can neither see nor hear nor move. And they did not repent (out) of their murders or their practice of magic (sorceries) or their sexual vice or their thefts."
(Rev. 9:20-21 Amp. Bible)

In these verses we are told that the people who survive this judgment are still unrepentant. They do not repent of the worship of the works of their own hands or their worship of demons. They do not repent of their worshipping of idols of gold, silver, bronze, stone or wood, which John says are things *"which neither can see nor hear nor move."* We are told that they continue to murder and practice magic, commit sexual sins and steal. This is a picture of total depravity and the total ignoring of the Word of God. Although there will be in those days many who will be Christians who will tell the Good News, it is evident that people will not repent.

2. Parenthetic Events

Just as there was an interlude or parenthetical period between the sixth and seventh seals, so there is between the sixth and seventh trumpet judgments. In this section, the parenthetical events that take place between the sixth and seventh trumpet judgments will be discussed. It must be understood that these events do not advance the chronology of the trumpet judgments.

a. Jews and Gentiles Saved During the Tribulation

"After this I saw four angels stationed at the four corners of the earth, firmly holding back the four winds of the earth, so that no wind should blow on the earth or sea or upon any tree. Then I saw a second angel coming up from the east (the rising of the sun), and carrying the seal of the living God. And with a loud voice he called out to the four angels who had been given the authority and power to injure the earth and sea, Saying, Harm not the earth nor the sea nor the trees, until we have sealed the bond servants of our God upon their foreheads." (Rev. 7:1-3 Amp. Bible)

I briefly mentioned this event earlier in the discussion about the fifth trumpet judgment under the subtitle "Demonic Torment of the Wicked." After the events of the sixth seal, we are told there were *"four angels stationed at the four corners of the earth, firmly holding back the four winds of the earth, so that no wind should blow on the earth or sea or upon any tree. Then I saw a second angel coming up from the east (the rising of the sun), and carrying the seal of the living God."* As stated earlier, this seal of God is to be placed upon the *"foreheads"* of God's people, to protect them from the judgments that are to come upon the earth. After God's people receive this seal, then the judgments continue in their consecutive order. At no time will the saints living on the earth during this terrible time of judgment be harmed by these judgments. The seal that is placed upon the *"foreheads"* of God's people is not said to be a visible seal. We do not know if it will be visible or not. However, God knows His people and He will protect them. Evidently the demons who will attack the wicked who dwell on the earth will be able to identify these that are sealed, for they are told to attack only those who *"do not have the seal (mark) of God on their foreheads."* (Rev. 9:4 Amp. Bible)

1. The 144,000 Out of Israel To Be Sealed

"And (then) I heard how many were sealed (marked) out of every tribe of the sons of Israel; there were a hundred and forty-four thousand sealed. Twelve thousand were sealed (marked) out of the tribe of Judah, twelve thousand out of the tribe of Reuben, twelve thousand out of the tribe of Gad, Twelve thousand out of the tribe of Asher, twelve thousand out of the tribe of Naphtali, twelve thousand out of the tribe of Manasseh, Twelve thousand out of the tribe of Simeon, twelve thousand out of the tribe of Levi, twelve thousand out of the tribe of Issachar, Twelve thousand out of the tribe of Zebulun, twelve thousand out of the tribe of Joseph, twelve thousand out of the tribe of Benjamin." (Rev. 7:4-8 Amp. Bible)

This scripture tells us that *"twelve thousand"* out of each of the twelve tribes *"of the sons of Israel"* are to receive this seal of *"the living God."* In Israel today, most Jewish people cannot say which tribe they belong to. But it is evident that God does know. These 144,000 that are to be sealed will be protected during the time of trials during the Tribulation period.

2. The Gentile Multitude

"After this I looked and a vast host appeared which no one could count, (gathered out) of every nation, from all tribes and peoples and languages. These stood before the throne and before the Lamb; they were attired in white robes, with palm branches in their hands. In loud voice they cried, saying, (Our) salvation is due to our God Who is seated on the throne, and to the Lamb—to Them (we owe our) deliverance." (Rev. 7:9-10 Amp. Bible)

In these verses John states that he sees *"a vast host,"* or great multitude, of people who are from every nation and language. This is a picture of many people which John says *"no one could count."* These are people from every nation throughout the world who have become Christians during the Tribulation period. The fact that they are *"attired in white robes"* is in reference to those in Rev. 6:11, who are the ones who have become martyrs because of their faith in God, which will be seen a little later in this chapter, i.e. vv. 13-14. The *"palm branches"* are in reference to the fact that they have gained the victory in that they have not compromised their faith. They ascribe praise to Jesus and to the Father and they acknowledge *"to Them (we owe our) deliverance!"* It is in these verses that we understand that there will be those who will become Christians during the Tribulation period. Many of these Tribulation saints will suffer death for their faith in God, while others will survive, because they have become sealed with the *"seal of the living God."* Those that have died as martyrs may have done so prior to the sealing of God's people. It is not said when or how these will die, but the fact is that they will die as martyrs and they will not deny God.

3. The Worship of the Heavenly Hosts

"And all the angels were standing round the throne and round the elders (of the heavenly Sanhedrin) and the four living creatures, and they fell prostrate before the throne and worshipped God. Amen! (So be it!) they cried. Blessing and glory and majesty and splendor and wisdom and thanks and honor and power and might (be ascribed) to our God to the ages and ages—forever and ever, throughout the eternities! Amen! (So be it!)" (Rev. 7:11-12 Amp. Bible)

Here we see that all the angels and the elders and the four living creatures join with the martyred saints in praise and worship unto God. They ascribe *"Blessing and glory and majesty and splendor and wisdom and thanks and honor and power and might"* to the God of all ages and all eternity, forever and ever. When we get to stand before God, I am sure that we too will be singing this praise to our God! He is worthy of all praise!

4. The Identification of the Gentile Multitude

"Then, addressing me, one of the elders (of the heavenly Sanhedrin) said, Who are these (people) clothed in the long white robes? And from where have they come? I replied, Sir, you know. And he said to me, These are they who have come out of the great tribulation (persecution), and have washed their robes and made them white in the blood of the Lamb." (Rev. 7:13-14 Amp. Bible)

As stated earlier, these are the people who have *"come out of the great tribulation."* These are the people who have become Christians during the Tribulation period and who have suffered death for their faith in God. In these verses, we are given affirmation of who these people are. We are told that they *"have washed their robes and made them white in the blood of the lamb."* It is the blood of Jesus that makes us clean. His blood covers our sins and we are made whole. It is His blood that will make our robes white and clean.

5. The Gentile Multitude Enjoy Rest

"For this reason they are (now) before the (very) throne of God, and serve Him day and night in his (temple) sanctuary; and He Who is sitting upon the throne will protect and spread His tabernacle over and shelter them with His presence. They shall hunger no more, neither thirst any more, neither shall the sun smite them, nor any scorching heat. For the Lamb Who is in the midst of the throne will be their Shepherd, and He will guide them to the springs of the waters of Life; and God shall wipe every tear away from their eyes." (Rev. 7:15-17 Amp. Bible)

In these verses we find the Gentile multitude who are martyrs giving praise and worship unto God and they serve

Him *"day and night."* We are given explanation of what God does for them; i.e. He protects them and takes away hunger and thirst. They will not feel the heat from the sun and God will wipe away all their tears. They will never tire or hunger or thirst again. In heaven there will be no need of sleep for our bodies will be changed and we will serve the Lord continually. Perhaps the fact that these are said to no longer have hunger or thirst or no longer will the *"sun smite them,"* thus they will feel no *"scorching heat,"* the suggestion would be that during life on earth they were tormented in these ways. They are now delivered from these things. The inference is that perhaps they had gone hungry rather than take the mark of the beast of Rev. 13. They very well could have been persecuted in these ways before death. Here we are told that God protects them and He feeds them and gives them rest.

b. The Mighty Angel And The Little Book

"Then I saw another mighty angel coming down from heaven, robed in a cloud, with a (halo like a) rainbow over his head; his face was like the sun, and his feet (legs) were like columns of fire. He had a little book (scroll) open in his hand. He set his right foot on the sea and his left foot on the land, And he shouted with a loud voice like the roaring of a lion; and when he had shouted, the seven thunders gave voice and uttered their message in distinct words. And when the seven thunders had spoken (sounded), I was going to write (it down), but I heard a voice from heaven saying, Seal up what the seven thunders have said! Do not write it down!" (Rev. 10:1-4 Amp. Bible)

This section is another parenthetical part of Revelation, and as stated earlier, these parenthetical sections do not advance the narrative of the events. Rather they contribute to the entire prophetic picture. As John is watching the vision that he sees, there comes forth *"another mighty angel."* Previously he would say that he had seen *"another angel,"* signifying that each of the angels that he saw were similar to each other. However, here he says that this angel is a *"mighty angel."* He goes on to describe what this angel looks like. He says that the angel is *"robed in a cloud, with a (halo like a) rainbow over his head; his face was like the sun, and his feet (legs) were like columns of fire."* Some people believe this *"mighty angel"* to be none other than Jesus. Others disagree on the basis that we are not told that Jesus will come to the earth or place His feet upon the earth until the end of the Tribulation period. It would seem more probable that this angel is created by God and given great power and authority and that he is a representative of God.

We are told that the *"mighty angel"* has in his hand *"a little book (scroll)"* and that it is open. We are not told what this little book is or what it contains. This angel, we are told, places one of his feet on the sea and the other on the land. He then *"shouted with a loud voice like the roaring of a lion."* John says that when this angel shouted, *"the seven thunders gave voice and uttered their message in distinct words."* We do not know and we are not told what these *"seven thunders"* are. Perhaps when we get to heaven, God will take the time to explain who or what they are to those of us that are interested. At any rate, we are told the *"seven thunders"* spoke a message in *"distinct words"* and that John was going to write down what they had said. However, he is told to *"Seal up what the seven thunders have said! Do not write it down!"* There have been those who have tried to say they know what the message was that the seven thunders had uttered. This cannot be possible, for John was told to seal up what they had said and not to write it down. Therefore, no one knows what they said, except John. He knew what they said, for he *"was going to write (it down)."* It is possible, however, that the *"seven thunders"* could have been another set of seven judgments that could have been more terrible still, but the sealing of them was significant of the shortening of the judgments. This, of course, is merely speculation. Perhaps when we get to heaven, God will reveal what the *"seven thunders"* said. I, for one, would like to know. However, it is evident that God did not want to reveal what they said as John was instructed to not write it down.

1. Announcement Of No Further Delay

"Then the (mighty) angel whom I had seen stationed on the sea and land raised his right hand to heaven (the sky), And swore in the name of (by) Him Who lives forever and ever, Who created the heavens (sky) and all they contain, and the earth and all that it contains, and the sea and all that it contains. (He swore) that no more time should intervene and there should be no more waiting or delay. But that when the days come that the trumpet call of the seventh angel is about to be sounded, then God's mystery—His secret design, His hidden purpose—as He had announced the glad tidings to His servants the prophets, should be fulfilled (accomplished, completed)." (Rev. 10:5-7 Amp. Bible)

In these verses, John notices that the *"mighty angel"* that he had seen *"stationed on the sea and land"* now raises his hand toward the sky and swears an oath. That we are told that this angel *"swore in the name of (by) Him Who lives forever and ever,"* implies that this angel cannot be Jesus and that God is much greater than he (the mighty angel) is.

In the oath we hear the angel say that *"no more time should intervene and there should be no more waiting or delay."* This does not mean, as some think, that the end of time is being proclaimed. Rather, it refers to the fact that time is about to run out and that there should be no delay. In other words, it is now the time when the remaining judgments are to be issued and that there should be no more delay. The end is to come soon, and the remaining judgments will come in rapid succession. We are told that *"when the days come that the trumpet call of the seventh angel is about to sound, then God's mystery—His secret design, His hidden purpose—as He had announced the glad tidings to His servants the prophets, should be fulfilled (accomplished, completed)."* The mystery referred to here is possibly the hidden secrets of God that have not been fully revealed to all. But when the seventh trumpet is sounded, God will bring about completion of His mystery. Soon, Jesus will come and He will establish His millennial kingdom on earth and perhaps in doing so, revealing God's hidden purpose. I'm sure that not everything about God has been revealed to mankind. But someday, we will know Him as He is.

2. John Commanded To Prophesy Again

"Then the voice that I heard from heaven spoke again to me, saying, Go and take the little book (scroll) which is open on the hand of the angel who is standing on the sea and on the land. So I went up to the angel and asked him to give me the little book. And he said to me, Take it and eat it. It will embitter your stomach, though in your mouth it will be sweet as honey. So I took the little book from the angel's hand and ate and swallowed it; it was sweet as honey in my mouth, but once I had swallowed it my stomach was embittered. Then they said to me, You are to make a fresh prophecy concerning many peoples and races and nations and languages and kings." (Rev. 10:8-11 Amp. Bible)

John says that he heard a voice from heaven speak to him which said, *"Go and take the little book (scroll) which is open on the hand of the angel who is standing on the sea and the land."* It is my opinion that this *"little book"* is more likely representative of the Word of God. In obedience, John did go to the angel and asked to be given the little book. He was told to *"Take it and eat it. It will embitter your stomach, though in your mouth it will be sweet as honey."* The Word of God is sweet to those who read its contents and is many times a blessing to us. But once we read it, sometimes the Word becomes bitter to us in the matter of persecutions that Christians sometimes experience. Furthermore, the eating of the *"little book"* is possibly representative of devouring the Word of God, or reading and obeying its contents. John said that he *"ate and swallowed it; it was sweet as honey in my mouth, but once I had swallowed it my stomach was embittered."* Undoubtedly, his persecution, which was imprisonment on the Isle of Patmos, was to him somewhat bitter. He knew he was there because of his faith and testimony of Christ.

Finally, John is told that he was to *"make a fresh prophecy concerning many peoples and races and nations and languages and kings."* This commandment that he is given to prophesy again is one that concerns the rest of the end time dealings with people and nations the world over. He will prophesy about the apostasies, persecutions and judgments that are quickly coming. This prophecy extends to a multitude of peoples, nations, languages and world leaders.

c. Times Of The Gentiles

"A Reed (as a measuring rod) was then given to me, (shaped) like a staff, and I was told: Rise up and measure the sanctuary of God and the altar (of incense), and (number) those who worship there; But leave out of your measuring the court outside the sanctuary of God; omit that, for it is given over to the Gentiles (the nations), and they will trample the holy city under foot for forty-two months (three and one-half years). (Rev. 11:1-2 Amp. Bible)

Revelation, chapter 11, continues with the parenthetical section that began earlier. This, again, does not advance the normal flow of the prophecies of Revelation. It merely adds to and helps to bring in better understanding of the events of the Apocalypse. Here, John is given a reed, or measuring rod, with which to measure the Temple of God. He is told to *"measure the sanctuary of God and the altar (of incense), and (number) those who worship there."* It would seem that God has instructed John to measure the area that belongs to Him in some special way. This area, the sanctuary and the altar, probably refers to the Holy Place and the Holy of Holies only. John is told to *"omit"* the outer court of the Temple, for this area, as well as the Holy City, Jerusalem, has been *"given over to the Gentiles (the nations), and they will trample the holy city under foot for forty-two months (three and one-half years)."* This Temple that John is to measure is most likely the Temple that is to be in existence during the Tribulation period. It will be allowed to be rebuilt for the purpose of allowing the Jews to renew their sacrifices and worshipping during the last days. But, as has been seen, the *"beast"* or Antichrist will enter into this Temple and set himself up as God and demand that people worship him as God.

The fact that we are told that the outer court and the city of Jerusalem, i.e., the *"holy city,"* is to be *"trampled under foot for forty-two months (three and one-half years)"* indicates that this will be during the last half of the Tribulation period, known as the Great Tribulation. Most of the judgments in Revelation are loosed upon the earth and those that dwell therein during this period. Some believe that this period of forty-two months, or three and one-half years, represents the first half of the Tribulation period. However, it seems more probable to be the last half of the period due to the fact that the *"covenant"* between Antichrist and the Jews at the beginning of the Tribulation period would allow the Jews considerable freedom during the first half of the period. It is in the middle of the final week of Daniel's prophecy of the *"Seventy weeks"* that Antichrist enters the Temple and breaks the *"covenant."* Afterwards, the Jews will not be allowed the freedom they enjoy during the first half of the period.

"They will fall by the sword and will be taken as prisoners to all the nations. Jerusalem will be trampled on by the Gentiles until the times of the Gentiles are fulfilled." (St. Luke 21:24 NIV)

In this verse, Jesus predicts the times of the Gentiles and how the Jews are to be treated during the last half of the Tribulation period. The *"times of the Gentiles are fulfilled"* will be when Jesus returns to set up His millennial kingdom on earth, at which time He will destroy all wickedness. Jesus will return to the earth at the close of the Tribulation period. This is also mentioned in the seventh trumpet judgment, which will be discussed a little later.

d. The Two Witnesses

"And I will give power to my two witnesses, and they will prophesy for 1260 days, clothed in sackcloth. These are the two olive trees and the two lampstands that stand before the Lord of the earth. If anyone tries to harm them, fire comes from their mouths and devours their enemies. This is how anyone who wants to harm them must die. These men have power to shut up the sky so that it will not rain during the time they are prophesying; and they have power to turn the waters into blood and to strike the earth with every kind of plague as often as they want." (Rev. 11: 3-6 NIV)

Through the years many preachers, teachers and writers have differed in belief as to who these *"two witnesses"* are. Some believe them to be Elijah and Enoch because neither of these two had tasted death, but were translated or "caught up" to Heaven. Others believe them to be Elijah and Moses because of the supernatural powers that these witnesses are said to have. Others have interpreted them to be the Church and Israel because of their witness on earth. However, I do not believe that either of these views could be correct.

Because Elijah and Enoch have not tasted physical death,

but were *"caught up"* to Heaven, some believe them to be the two witnesses spoken of here in Revelation 11. They believe that these two men of God will come back to earth and minister for three and one-half years, then be killed and come back to life and rise to be with Jesus. But not all people are going to die a physical death, as was seen in Chapter Two of this book concerning the Rapture of the Church. There are going to be many who will be alive on the earth at the time when Jesus comes *"in the air"* and gathers His Church unto Himself. Those who are alive on the earth at that time will be *"caught up"* in much the same manner as was Elijah and Enoch. Although Elijah was caught up in a *"chariot of fire"* (2 Kings 2:11) and Enoch just disappeared and *"was not found, because God translated him,"* (Heb. 11:5) the intent was not to bring them back at a later time in order to suffer death. Therefore, it cannot possibly be either Elijah or Enoch who are the two witnesses.

Elijah and Moses cannot be the two witnesses, as some believe. Elijah cannot be for the reasons stated above. Moses is thought to be the other witness due to the fact that he appeared with Elijah at the time of the transfiguration. (St. Matt. 17:3) Also, he is considered as one of the witnesses because of Jude 9, where we are told that the Archangel, Michael, fought with the devil for Moses' body. I contend that Moses cannot be one of the witnesses due to the fact that he has died a physical death already. Hebrews 9:27 states that *"It is appointed unto men once to die."* Why would God allow Moses to die and then come back to earth as one of the witnesses and then suffer death a second time?

Although the two witnesses spoken of in chapter 11 are said to have certain powers resembling that of the powers that both Elijah and Moses possessed during their lifetime on earth, it does not mean that these two or any other Old or New Testament personage can be the witnesses. It is entirely possible that God can use two men who are alive during the

Tribulation period, and endow them with whatever powers He determines to give them. This is more preferable to accept than that of one of the great heroes of old.

These witnesses are to *"prophesy 1260 days."* This period of 1260 days is the same as the *"forty-two months"* or the three and one-half years, or the last half, of the Tribulation period. During this last half of the period the witnesses are said to be able to *"shut up the sky so that it will not rain..."* They will be able to *"turn the waters into blood and to strike the earth with every kind of plague as often as they want."* The two witnesses will be able to minister to people and bring certain judgments into play as often as they deem it necessary. They will be able to destroy those who try to harm them in any way. We are told that if *"anyone tries to harm them, fire comes from their mouths and devours their enemies."* We can see a parallel whereas in the ministry of Elijah, he called fire down from heaven and destroyed two thirds of the company of soldiers sent to arrest him. The remaining soldiers were spared only because they pleaded with Elijah for their lives. (2 Kings 1) Therefore, the two witnesses will be able to withstand their enemies the entire three and one-half years of their ministry. It will only be when their ministry is completed that their enemies will be able to have a temporary victory over them.

1. The Death Of The Two Witnesses

"Now when they have finished their testimony, the beast that comes up from the Abyss will attack them, and overpower and kill them. Their bodies will lie in the street of the great city, which is figuratively called Sodom and Egypt, where also their Lord was crucified. For three and a half days men from every people, tribe, language and nation will gaze on their bodies and refuse them burial. The inhabitants of the earth will gloat over them and will celebrate by

sending each other gifts, because these two prophets had tormented those who live on the earth." (Rev. 11:7-10 NIV)

We are told that *"when they have finished their testimony"* they were overpowered and killed by the *"beast that comes up out of the Abyss."* Prior to this, the two witnesses were able to withstand anyone who tried to harm them in any way. During their three and one-half years of ministry, they will be untouched and unharmed. However, once their ministry is completed, God will allow them to become overpowered and killed.

This *"beast that comes up out of the Abyss"* is none other than Satan. When we speak of the *"beast"* out of the sea, it is in reference to Antichrist, whereas, the *"beast"* who comes up out of the land is in reference to the false prophet. But it is Satan, the *"beast that comes up out of the Abyss"* that will make war with the two witnesses and will successfully subdue, or kill them. The victory that Satan has over the witnesses is so great that the people of the world who were *"tormented"* by their ministry and their miracles which they perform, will not allow their bodies to be buried. They will cause their bodies to lie in the street to be looked upon and perhaps scoffed at for a period of *"three and a half days."* During this time, we are told that the people celebrate the fact that the witnesses are dead and they send gifts to one another. It seems that by now the people believe that their fear of God and His wrath and power is no longer warranted. They believe that they have gotten the victory over their common enemy since these two witnesses are now dead. No longer will they be tormented with plagues, they believe. This is for them a happy occasion.

The ministry of the two witnesses began in the middle of the Tribulation period. It lasts for 1260 days, or three and a half years. Therefore, if their ministry is now finished, it signifies the end of the final week of Daniel's prophecy of the *"Seventy weeks."* This means that there are but only a few days when Jesus will come and end all rebellion and put an end to all sin. He will soon come to establish His kingdom on the earth.

2. The Resurrection Of The Two Witnesses

"But after the three and a half days a breath of life from God entered them, and they stood on their feet, and terror struck those who saw them. Then they heard a loud voice from heaven saying to them, "Come up here." And they went up to heaven in a cloud, while their enemies looked on. At that very hour there was a severe earthquake and a tenth of the city collapsed. Seven thousand people were killed in the earthquake, and the survivors were terrified and gave glory to the God of heaven." (Rev. 11:11-13 NIV)

While the people are rejoicing over the death of the witnesses, at the end of the *"three and a half days,"* suddenly the witnesses come back to life and stand to their feet. We are told that *"terror struck those who saw them."* Imagine that you are looking at two men who have been killed and have been lying in the street for three and a half days. You know without a doubt that they are dead. Perhaps you even got a close look and perhaps touched them to ensure that they were dead. But suddenly, as you are looking at them, they stand up and are alive and breathing just as though they had not died. This scene would strike terror in most people! It is not said, but one can imagine that perhaps some with weak hearts would suddenly die with heart attacks. This scene would be a shock almost beyond belief!

Just as suddenly, the people who are watching this unusual scene before them hear a voice from heaven saying, *"Come up here."* While they are watching, before their very eyes, they see these two men, these whom they had feared for three and a half years, these whom they were celebrating because they were dead, suddenly go up into heaven *"in a cloud"* as they are watching! This would cause me to fall upon my knees and cry out to God for His mercy and forgiveness!

When the witnesses are *"caught up"* to heaven, we are told that a *"severe earthquake"* shook the area and a *"tenth of the city collapsed."* The city named here is called *"Sodom and Egypt."* It is, however, the city of Jerusalem, for we are told that it was where the Lord was crucified. We are told that seven thousand people will be killed in the earthquake. There is no reason to not take these numbers literally. In this day and time, we have had many earthquakes in various parts of the world and literally thousands of people have died as a result. Whole cities have been completely destroyed. Therefore, it is entirely possible that a tenth of Jerusalem will be literally destroyed and literally seven thousand people will be killed in this great earthquake.

As stated earlier, I think that if I were a sinner and saw the events of such grandeur as in these verses, I would be on my knees crying out to God for His mercy and forgiveness. We are told that the people give *"glory to the God of heaven."* They acknowledge that God is the true God and that He is greater and more powerful that any pagan god. However, we are not told that they commit their lives to Christ.

e. Prominent Personages

In Revelation 12, we are introduced to five personages who are the "actors" of the Tribulation period. This is another parenthetical section, which as stated before, does not advance the normal flow of the book, but rather they add to the understanding of it. These personages are (1) the woman, who represents Israel, (2) the dragon, representative of Satan, (3) the man-child, representing Christ, (4) Michael, who represents the angels, and (5) Israel, the remnant seed of the woman. In the next section of this book, (subtitle f), and in the thirteenth chapter of Revelation, we will be introduced to two more prominent personages. These will be Antichrist and the false prophet. But first, the woman, who represents Israel will be discussed.

1.The Woman: Israel

"A great and wondrous sign appeared in heaven: a woman clothed with the sun, with the moon under her feet and a crown of twelve stars on her head. She was pregnant and cried out in pain as she was about to give birth." (Rev. 12:1-2 NIV)

In these verses we are told that John sees a *"great and wondrous sign"* which is a *"woman clothed with the sun, with the moon under her feet and a crown of twelve stars on her head."* Many have said that this *"sign"* is none other than the Church. Others state that it is Christ. However, this is neither the Church nor Christ. This sign is representative of Israel. We are told in the second verse that the woman is *"pregnant and cried out in pain as she was about to give birth."* Jesus, who is the *"man-child,"* which will be discussed a little later, was born in Bethlehem, Israel. These verses are a picture of the place where Jesus was born. The *"twelve stars"* are representative of the twelve tribes of Israel.

The fact that we are told that the *"woman"* cries out in pain is logical of the fact that after Jesus was born, Herod had all the children two years of age and under killed in an attempt to kill Christ. (St. Matt. 2:16-18) The travailing in pain which the *"woman"* in these verses is said to be experiencing also may be representative of the fact that during the Tribulation period, Israel will endure many trials. The people in Israel will suffer hunger and even death because of the trials she will endure.

2. The Red Dragon: Satan

"Then another sign appeared in heaven: an enormous red dragon with seven heads and ten horns and seven crowns on his heads. His tail swept a third of the stars out of the sky and flung them to the earth. The dragon stood in front of the woman who was about to give birth, so that he might devour her child the moment it was born." (Rev. 12:3-4 NIV)

Here we are told that *"an enormous red dragon with seven heads and ten horns and seven crowns on his heads"* stands before the *"woman"* awaiting the birth of the *"man-child."* This *"red dragon"* is representative of the Revised Roman Empire. During the study of the formation of the Revised Roman Empire, I said that within this empire ten kingdoms would come into existence. One of the kings of one of the ten kingdoms will war against and *"subdue"* three other kingdoms within this empire. When this war is over, the Revived Grecian Empire will have come into power. The remaining six kingdoms of the Revised Roman Empire will give their power and authority to Antichrist, who is the king of the Revived Grecian Empire. Therefore, the *"ten horns"* are representative of the ten kingdoms of the Revised Roman Empire **before** the Revived Grecian Empire comes into power. The *"seven heads"* and the *"seven crowns"* are representative of the kings of the six remaining kingdoms of the Revised Roman Empire, and the king of the Revived Grecian Empire.

In Rev. 12:9, the *"red dragon"* is named as Satan. It is clear that the *"red dragon"* in this verse is representative of both the empire of Antichrist and of the satanic power unleashed in the world during the Tribulation Period. We are told that the tail of the dragon *"swept a third of the stars out of the sky and flung them to the earth."* There are those who have stated that the *"third of the stars"* is representative of the number of angels who were cast out of heaven at the time that Satan is cast out. However, at no time does scripture number the angels that were on the side of Satan and who were cast out with him. We are only told that *"his angels were cast out with him."* Far more preferable is it to understand that the *"third of the stars"* refers to those who oppose Satan both politically and spiritually during the Tribulation period.

The dragon is pictured as standing in front of the woman *"so that he might devour her child the moment it was born."* Again, this is representative of when Jesus was born in Bethlehem, Herod had all children two years of age and under killed in an attempt to destroy Christ. It may further indicate that the Jews who do not obey the command to receive the mark and worship Antichrist as God will be captured and put to death.

3.The Male Child: Christ

"She gave birth to a son, a male child, who will rule all the nations with an iron scepter. And her child was snatched up to God and to His throne. The woman fled into the desert to a place prepared for her by God, where she might be taken care of for 1260 days." (Rev. 12:5-6 NIV)

The *"woman"* in verses one and two is representative of Israel. Israel was destined to bring forth the *"male child,"* Christ, to rule all the nations of the world, which will come into place at the time of the Millennial period. However, He was *"snatched up to God and to his throne,"* or in other words, He ascended into Heaven to God's throne where He awaits the time to come to the earth to establish His kingdom. Some people think the *"male child"* is representative of the Church. But it was Christ who ascended to God and to His throne, not the Church. When Jesus returns for the Church, they are taken to heaven for the purpose of receiving their rewards and becoming married to Christ. Before the Rapture, the Church is considered to be the bride waiting for the return of the bridegroom.

In verse five we see the picture of Christ being *"caught up"* to the throne of God. Then in verse six, the *"woman,"* or mother of the male child, flees into the *"desert,"* or wilderness, to a *"place prepared for her by God, where she might be taken care of for 1260 days."* The fact that there is a tremendous period of time from the birth to the ascension, then to the *"woman"* fleeing into the desert, indicates that this is not an uncommon occurrence in prophecy. The *"woman"* flees to a place where she is to be cared for by God for a period of 1260 days. This period of time is the same as the last three a half years of the Tribulation period. I stated earlier that a remnant of Israel will flee to a place perhaps in Jordan called Petra, or Sela. The *"desert"* spoken of here in this verse is the same as the prediction earlier stated.

4. The Archangel: Michael

"And there was war in heaven. Michael and his angels fought against the dragon, and the dragon and his angels fought back. But he was not strong enough, and they lost their place in heaven. The great dragon was hurled down—that ancient serpent called the devil, or Satan, who leads the whole world astray. He was hurled to the earth, and his angels with him. Then I heard a loud voice in heaven say: "Now have come the salvation and the power and the kingdom of our God, and the authority of his Christ. For the accuser of our brothers, who accuses them before our God day and night, has been hurled down. They overcame him by the blood of the Lamb and by the word of their testimony; they did not love their lives so much as to shrink from death. Therefore rejoice, you heavens and you who dwell in them! But woe to the earth and the sea, because the devil has gone down to you! He is filled with fury, because he knows that his time is short." (Rev. 12:7-12 NIV)

In the book of Daniel we are told, *"And at that time shall Michael stand up, the great prince who standeth for the children of thy people, and there shall be a time of trouble, such as never was since there was a nation even to that same time; and at that time thy people shall be delivered, every one that shall be found written in the book."* (Dan. 12:1) Michael is the angel, or *"prince"* who fights for God's people. We are told that there will be war in heaven. Some believe this war to be in the universe, such as the sky or stars, similar to a star war portrayed in Hollywood. However, this war will actually be fought in the presence of God. We are told that Satan is the accuser of the brothers and that he accuses them before God *"day and night."* We know that Satan goes before the throne of God to accuse us because of what we are told in Job 1:6-12. During this war, Satan will lose and he and his angels are to be cast into the earth. Once Satan is cast into the earth, he will be *"filled with fury, because he knows his time is short."* It will be at this time when he will unleash all of his satanic power upon the inhabitants of the earth. He will no longer have access to the throne of God. He will only be able to operate within the limits of the earth and the sky and space, i.e., stars and other planets.

This war in heaven and the casting of Satan into the earth all coincides with the beginning of the last half of the Tribulation period. It predates the opening of the Seven Seals. Most all of Revelation from chapter 4:1 and forward pertains to the last half of the Tribulation period. This will be the time when Antichrist enters the Temple of the Jews and demands that he be worshipped as God. Also, it will be at this time when people will be given the choice to either receive the mark of Antichrist or be subject to death. The first half of the Tribulation period, although there will be war throughout its duration, will be relatively mild compared to what happens when Satan is cast into the earth for the last half of the period.

John hears a *"voice in heaven"* that says *"Now have come salvation....for the accuser of our brothers...has been hurled down."*

As has been stated before, it is not uncommon to go from one point of time in prophecy to another point of time in prophecy. The same is true here. Satan is cast out of heaven at the middle of the Tribulation period, or at the beginning of the last half of the period; then we are told that *"salvation"* has come. This statement refers to deliverance. Although the *"voice in heaven"* is not identified, it would seem that it belongs to possibly the Tribulation saints who have long anticipated victory. Therefore, it seems that the Tribulation saints, who were killed for their testimony of Christ, shout victory and sing a song of deliverance because they have overcome Satan by the blood of the Lamb.

The voice continues to speak and pronounces *"woe to the earth and the sea, because the devil has gone down to you!"* Satan is said to be *"filled with fury"* for he knows that his time remaining is short. At the time when this pronouncement is made, Satan will have only a few days to unleash whatever *"fury"* he may have. He knows that he will lose the war with God. Believe me, Satan knows the outcome just as well as we do. He knows that he will be destroyed soon and he will unleash every satanic evil that he can possibly conceive during his final days.

5. Israel: The Remnant Seed Of The Woman

"When the dragon saw that he had been hurled to the earth, he pursued the woman who had given birth to the male child. The woman was given the two wings of a great eagle, so that she might fly to the place prepared for her in the desert, where she would be taken care of for a time, times and half a time, out of the serpent's reach. Then from his mouth the serpent spewed water like a river, to overtake the woman and sweep her away with the torrent. But the earth helped the woman by opening its mouth and swallowing the river that the dragon had spewed out of his mouth. Then the dragon was enraged at the woman and went off to make war against the rest

of her offspring — those who obey God's commandments and hold to the testimony of Jesus." (Rev. 12:13-17 NIV)

Satan is like a spoiled angry bully who, because he is cast out of heaven, goes after the one he believes to be the cause of his trouble. Israel, the *"woman,"* brought forth the *"male child"* Who is none other than Jesus. As soon as Satan is cast into the earth, he begins to *"pursue"* Israel. This, again, is the scene of Antichrist, being led by Satan, who enters into the Temple and sets himself up as God and demands that all Jews and people throughout his territory worship him as God. When this happens, many of the Jews will flee Israel. As stated before, they will flee to a place called Petra or Sela in Jordan. It will be here that they will stay for a *"time, times and half a time"*, or three and a half years.

We are told that the *"woman"* will be given *"the two wings of an eagle, so that she might fly to the place prepared for her in the desert."* It is not said what this refers to. However, it could be that by some miracle, God will allow a large group of Jewish people to fly out of Israel to Jordan by aircraft, possibly somehow undetected by Antichrist or his military. Howsoever this will be done, Antichrist, who is taken over by Satan, will be enraged and will spew *"water"* out of his mouth *"like a river, to overtake the woman and sweep her away with the torrent."* Some believe the *"water"* means a literal flood of some sort. However, it is more plausible to understand it to be a military force sent out to overtake fleeing Israel. However, God will intervene on behalf of Israel, and we are told that the earth will open its mouth and swallow the river. Therefore, it would seem that the military sent to overtake Israel will be destroyed in some miraculous way by God. This will, of course, only anger Satan all the more. We are told that he will become *"enraged at the woman and went off to make war against her offspring."* Israel's *"offspring"* in this case are those who were not able to flee Israel. They will be there to endure the

E. RICHARD BRIDGEFORTH, SR.

trials of the last half of the Tribulation period. Although many will be killed for their testimony in Christ, many will still be alive at the time of Jesus' Second Coming to establish His earthly kingdom.

Verse 17 in this prophecy says that the *"dragon was enraged at the woman and went off to make war against her offspring."* This verse looks forward to the end of the Tribulation period just before Jesus' Second Coming to the earth. Antichrist now has a reason to bring in all of his military to destroy Israel. Also, Antichrist will bring in the military of the nations who ally themselves with him to do battle against Israel. But it really isn't Israel that the *"dragon"* is thinking about here. The *"dragon"* (Satan) knows that Jesus is coming to establish His earthly kingdom. Therefore, this is a front to wage war against Jesus with the foolish hope that he and his armies will be able to prevent Jesus from being able to establish His kingdom on earth.

f. The Antichrist And False Prophet

Another parenthetical section in Revelation is introduced in chapter thirteen. Once again, I want to reiterate that these parenthetical sections do not advance the narrative of Revelation. They merely point out to us different characters, places or events that add to our understanding of the normal flow of the book. In this chapter of Revelation, we are introduced to two characters that have a starring role throughout the Tribulation period. They are the beast that comes up out of the sea, Antichrist, and the beast that comes up out of the land, the false prophet.

1. Antichrist: The Beast Out Of The Sea

"And I stood upon the sand of the sea, and saw a beast rise up out of the sea, having seven heads and ten horns, and upon his horns ten crowns, and upon his heads the name of blasphemy. And the beast which I saw was like a leopard, and his feet were like the feet of a bear, and his mouth like the mouth of a lion; and the dragon gave him his power, and his throne, and great authority." (Rev. 13:1-2)

In these verses we see the Revised Roman Empire in its entirety. This *"beast"* is said to have *"seven heads and ten horns, and upon his horns ten crowns."* The Roman Empire was first established in Rome. Due to the fact that there were seven mountains surrounding the area, we know that the old Roman Empire was headquartered in Rome. In this scene, the beast has ten horns and ten crowns, which is suggestive of the original ten kingdoms, and their kings that make up the Revised Roman Empire. As stated earlier, one of the kings of one of the ten kingdoms rises up and wages war against three other kingdoms within the Revised Roman Empire. He will *"subdue"* these three kingdoms, and he, Antichrist, will be the ruler over his kingdom and the three that he subdues. This will make up the Revived Grecian Empire.

The fact that we are told that we see *"upon his heads the name of blasphemy,"* is most likely to mean that this *"beast,"* the Revised Roman Empire, over which Antichrist becomes ruler, is in opposition to God. The kings of each of the kingdoms of this empire will be against God and all that He stands for.

In verse two, we are told that the *"beast"* has the characteristics *"like a leopard, and his feet were like the feet of a bear, and his mouth like the mouth of a lion."* In Daniel, we are told that the third beast that Daniel had seen in his vision was *"like a leopard."* (Dan. 7:6) This was representative of the Grecian Empire, whose king was Alexander the Great. The *"he-goat"* in Daniel 8:3-8 was also representative of the Grecian Empire. The fact that we are told here in Revelation 13:2 that this beast which rises up out of the sea has the characteristics like a leopard, is indicative that the old Grecian Empire has been revived. The *"sea"* is representative of perhaps a great mass of people, namely the Gentile world powers, and also possibly from the Mediterranean area. This would be true in that Antichrist does come from the Mediterranean area, namely the Syrian Kingdom, and this is a Gentile nation. As stated in the previous paragraph, Antichrist will win a war against three kingdoms within the Revised Roman Empire, thus, causing the Grecian Empire to be revived.

We are told that the *"beast"* has *"the feet of a bear, and his mouth like the mouth of a lion."* This indicates that Antichrist will have the majesty of a lion, the tenacity of a bear and the swiftness of a leopard, which were the characteristics of Alexander the Great during his conquests. In addition to these characteristics, we are told that the *"dragon,"* or Satan, gives Antichrist his *"power, and his throne, and great authority."* Therefore, Antichrist will have great power given to him by Satan and will rule with satanic power.

a. The Deadly Wound

"And I saw one of his heads as though it were wounded to death; and his deadly wound was healed, and all the world wondered after the beast." (Rev, 13:3)

There have been many different interpretations of this verse. Some believe that this head that is *"wounded to death"* but was healed, or comes back to life, suggests that some historic person is raised back to life and therefore it will be this person that will be Antichrist. Others favor more modern personalities such as Hitler or Stalin. It is more plausible to interpret this verse as the revival of the Grecian Empire. Most people believe the Grecian Empire to be dead and will no longer be seen or heard from. Some believe it will be the Roman Empire that will be revived. However, scriptures point to the revival of the Grecian Empire, as has been stated earlier in this study. The Grecian Empire will be revived and will come into existence again and will amaze many people throughout the world. Antichrist, as has been discovered, will be the ruler of the Revived Grecian Empire, as well as eventually over the Revised Roman Empire. When the *"beast"* is referred to in this chapter, it is both the Revived Grecian Empire and the person who is ruler over the empire, Antichrist, which is being referred to. It is not the person, the human ruler, who is dead and comes back to life. Rather, it is the empire itself.

b. The Satanic Worship

"And they worshipped the dragon who gave power unto the beast; and they worshipped the beast, saying, Who is like the beast? Who is able to make war with him?" (Rev. 13:4)

Here we are told that the people throughout the world *"worshipped the dragon who gave power unto the beast; and they worshipped the beast."* When Antichrist enters the Jewish Temple during the middle of the seventieth week, the Tribulation period, he will defile the Temple and set himself up as God. He will demand the worship of people throughout his kingdom, the Revived Grecian Empire, and the Revised Roman Empire, and others who ally themselves with him. He will state that he is God! Thus, he is Satan's Christ in whom he has given his power and throne and authority. Therefore, it is in the beginning of the last half of the Tribulation period when this scene takes place.

The question is asked, *"Who is like the beast? Who is able to make war with him?"* People throughout the world will believe that no other nation or kingdom will be able to stand against Antichrist. However, he will be at war during the last half of the Tribulation period as was seen earlier. He will be at war with the countries *"out of the east and out of the north."* (Dan. 11:44) It will take Antichrist most the entire last half of the Tribulation period to win this war. He then will enter into another war against Israel, but end up in a war against Jesus at His Second Coming. It will be Jesus Who will be the answer to the question the people ask. Jesus will defeat Antichrist and cast him into the lake of fire. Satan, as will be seen later, will be bound in the Abyss for a thousand years. At any rate, it will be Jesus, Who will have the power to overthrow Antichrist and his government, as well as Satan himself.

c. The Evil Character Of The Beast

"And there was given unto him a mouth speaking great things and blasphemies, and power was given unto him to continue forty and two months. And he opened his mouth in blasphemy against God, to blaspheme his name, and his tabernacle, and them in heaven. And it was given unto him to make war with the saints, and to overcome them; and power was given him over all kindreds and tongues and nations. And all that dwell upon the earth shall worship him, whose names are not written in the book of life of the Lamb slain from the foundation of the world." (Rev. 13:5-8)

We are told that the *"beast,"* Antichrist, speaks *"great things and blasphemies."* He blasphemes against God and His name and those that are in heaven. Antichrist is a boastful person and he gains attention to himself in this manner. When Antichrist first comes into power, he does so possibly before the beginning of the Tribulation period. However, at that time, he comes as a mild and meek individual in order to deceive many. He makes a peace treaty, or *"covenant,"* with Israel to protect them, possibly while they rebuild the Temple and begin their sacrifices and worship. He will completely fool people throughout the world. But at the time he enters into the Temple and demands that all worship him as God, he then shows his true evil character.

Once Antichrist reveals his true character, he is given *"forty and two months"* to wage war and to come against the saints. This *"forty and two months"* is the same as the last three and a half years of the Tribulation period. We are told that he will *"overcome"* the saints. Many saints of God, who have given their hearts to Christ after the Rapture of the Church, will be killed for their faith in God. There will be many other saints who will escape death because they receive God's seal, and others are kept safe by fleeing from Israel. But thousands of saints will be put to death because they will not worship the *"beast"* or receive his mark.

We are told that all who *"dwell upon the earth shall worship him, whose names are not written in the book of life of the Lamb slain from the foundation of the world."* Every person who will not repent and turn to God during the Tribulation period will worship the *"beast."* This includes every nation that is allied with Antichrist, as well as those nations who are just caught up by his majesty. Some people believe that the entire world, every nation and all peoples throughout the world will be under the power of Antichrist. Antichrist **will only** rule over the Revised Roman Empire and the Revived Grecian Empire. He will have power over the nations who ally themselves with him. But the nations that do not ally themselves with Antichrist will not be under his dictatorship. However, there will be literally thousands in every nation throughout the world who will be influenced by Antichrist, and thus, they will worship him. Only those whose names are not found *"written in the book of life of the Lamb"* will be deceived and worship the *"beast."* This includes the unsaved Jews and Gentiles throughout the world.

d. The Exhortation to Hear

"If any man have an ear, let him hear. He that leadeth into captivity shall go into captivity; he that killeth with the sword must be killed with the sword. Here is the patience and the faith of the saints." (Rev. 13:9-10)

Here we are invited to hear what the Word is telling us. We are told that those who lead others into captivity will themselves be led into captivity. Those who kill by a certain means, they too will be killed. Those who lead others astray and who kill will be faced with being found out of the will of God and they will face His judgments. Many sinners will die during the last half of the Tribulation period because of their treatment of the saints and because they fail to except God. The saints must keep faith and patience in God in order to receive His blessings. They must not give in to the hardships and trials that the wicked present them with. Those that endure, though many will be killed, will enter into the joys of the Lord.

2. The False Prophet: The Beast Out Of The Land

"And I beheld another beast coming up out of the earth; and he had two horns like a lamb, and spoke like a dragon. And he exerciseth all the power of the first beast before him, and causeth the earth and them who dwell on it to worship the first beast, whose deadly wound was healed." (Rev. 13:11-12)

John now sees a second *"beast coming up out of the earth."* The fact that he is said to come up out of the earth is representative of his being a creature of the earth rather than of heaven. We are told that he has *"two horns like a lamb."* This indicates that he is a religious leader of sorts. However, he speaks *"as a dragon,"* which is suggestive that he is led by

Satan. This is the identification of none other than the False Prophet. This *"beast"* is the religious leader of an Apostate religion.

We are told that this second beast *"exerciseth all the power of the first beast before him."* This is an indication that he is empowered to impose laws to make the people worship the first beast, Antichrist. Antichrist will come on the scene at the beginning of the Tribulation period, when he makes the *"covenant"* with Israel. So also will the False Prophet, who will be the head of the Apostate religion during this period. Although the Apostate Church will be destroyed according to Revelation 17:6, the False Prophet will survive this destruction and be available to bring about the final Apostate religion of worshipping Antichrist during the last half of the Tribulation period.

a. The Miracles Performed By The False Prophet

"And he doeth great wonders, so that he maketh fire come down from heaven on the earth in the sight of men, And deceiveth them that dwell on the earth by the means of those miracles which he had power to do in the sight of the beast, saying to them that dwell on the earth, that they should make an image to the beast, that had the wound by a sword and did live." (Rev. 13:13-14)

We are told that the False Prophet does *"great wonders, so that he maketh fire come down from heaven on the earth in the sight of men."* That Satan is able to perform certain miracles is true. This was seen when Moses went before Pharaoh to seek for the release of the Israelites. We are told that Moses said to Aaron, *"Take thy rod, and cast it before Pharaoh, and it shall become a serpent."* When Aaron did this, we are told that the *"magicians of Egypt, they also did in like manner with their enchantments. For they cast down every man his rod, and they became serpents."* (Ex. 7:8-13) Therefore, although the rod of

Aaron became a serpent, which was a miracle that God enabled Aaron and Moses to perform, the magicians of Egypt were also able to perform the same kind of miracle by Satan's power. It was through Satan that the magicians of Egypt received their power to perform miracles. It will also be through Satan that the False Prophet will be empowered to perform miracles. However, the people of the earth will be deceived by the miracles performed by the False Prophet. They will think he is of God and that what he says is truly from God. By his deception, he will cause an image of the first beast to be made so that all the people throughout the world will worship Antichrist.

b. The Law Imposed For All To Worship The Beast

"And he hath power to give life unto the image of the beast, that the image of the beast should both speak, and cause that as many as would not worship the image of the beast should be killed. And he causeth all, both small and great, rich and poor, free and enslaved, to receive a mark in their right hand, or in their foreheads, And that no man might buy or sell, except he that had the mark, or the name of the beast, or the number of his name." (Rev. 13: 15-17)

It is not known what the *"image of the beast"* will be. Some say it will be nothing more than a robot. Others have ideas that it could be a clone of Antichrist. Whatever the *"image of the beast"* shall be, we are told that the False Prophet has the power to give life unto the image. He will cause it to speak and it will be so convincing that the people of the earth will accept it and what it says, and they will worship the first beast, Antichrist. With the advanced scientific technologies of today, this would not be a hard task to accomplish.

The *"image of the beast"* causes many people throughout the earth to worship Antichrist. We are told that those who do not worship Antichrist must be killed. Undoubtedly, there will be many that will die for not worshipping Antichrist, as intimated in Rev. 7: 9-17 that there will be many martyrs during the Tribulation period. However, because of the war that will be ongoing between Antichrist and the countries *"out of the east and out of the north,"* (Dan. 11: 44) the execution of this law that those who do not worship the beast must be killed will not be totally fulfilled. Many will escape this law and survive to the end of the Tribulation period.

We are told that all that worship the beast must receive a mark in either their right hand or their foreheads to enable them to buy or sell. This mark will be a sign to others that those that have this mark are worshippers of the beast and it will serve as a source of identification. Those that do not have the mark will not be able to buy or sell and they will be singled out and killed by those who do have the mark. It will be a means of forcing people to worship the beast. However, as stated earlier, many will not take this mark and they will escape death and survive to the end of the Tribulation period.

c. The Mark Of The Beast

"Here is wisdom. Let him that hath understanding count the number of the beast; for it is the number of a man; and his number is six hundred threescore and six." (Rev. 13:18)

What is the mark of the beast? Many have tried to say what the mark will be. It is not known what the mark will be. Some have said that with today's technologies, a small microchip can be placed just under the skin and with such a device, it could be scanned thereby allowing people to be able to buy or sell. Others say it would seem more probable that whatever the mark will be, it would need to be visible for all to see. Whatever the mark will be, we know that if received in the right hand or in the forehead, the person receiving the mark will be doomed to Hell. Those receiving the mark have sealed their doom because, by taking the mark, they have decided to worship the beast.

We are told that the number of the beast *"is the number of a man."* Many have tried to calculate various numbers to come up with the name of Antichrist. By virtue of arranging the numbers of different letters of the alphabet to coincide with the number 666, some try to say that Antichrist will be some character of Biblical times brought back to life. The fact that Antichrist will be a man is true. However, it is far more probable that he will be a man of modern times rather than some Biblical character brought back to life. The number 666 is, in my opinion, that it *"is the number of a man."* It is short of perfection. Man can never reach perfection no matter how he tries. Therefore, I submit that the number 666 is not the mark of the beast as some suggest, but rather, it is only the imperfect number of mankind.

g. The Lamb And The 144,000 On Mount Zion

"Then I looked, and there before me was the Lamb, standing on Mount Zion, and with him 144,000 who had his name and his Father's name written on their foreheads. And I heard a sound from heaven like the roar of rushing waters and like a loud peal of thunder. The sound I heard was like that of harpists playing their harps. And they sang a new song before the throne and before the four living creatures and the elders. No one could learn the song except the 144,000 who had been redeemed from the earth. These are those who did not defile themselves with women, for they kept themselves pure. They follow the Lamb wherever he goes. They were purchased from among men and offered as firstfruits to God and the Lamb. No lie was found in their mouths; they are blameless." (Rev. 14:1-5 NIV)

Revelation 14 brings about the conclusion of the parenthetical events. As has been stated throughout, these events do not advance the narrative of Revelation, however, they add to the understanding of the book as a whole. Once this chapter is finished, the chronological events will be resumed with the sounding of the seventh trumpet judgment. There is one other interlude, or parenthetical section that will be discussed a little later, after the seventh bowl judgment.

In the above verses we are introduced to *"the Lamb, standing on Mount Zion, and with him 144,000 who had his name and his Father's name written on their foreheads."* The *"Lamb"* is in reference to none other than Jesus. We are told that He is standing on Mount Zion. Many have the idea that Mount Zion is the heavenly city of Jerusalem and that it is in Heaven where this particular event takes place. The 144,000 are explained to be those who were sealed in Revelation, chapter seven, and that they are now resurrected and standing with Jesus in Heaven in the New Jerusalem. However, this cannot be the meaning of these verses.

The 144,000 **are** the same group that was sealed in chapter seven. However, they are not resurrected, as some believe. They are alive and well, standing with Jesus. We are told that at the time of Jesus' return to the earth, He will *"stand on the Mount of Olives, east of Jerusalem."* (Zech. 14:4) It is my contention that the Mount of Olives and Mount Zion are really both one and the same. Therefore, the verses above are a scene of Jesus and the 144,000 standing on the *"Mount of Olives, east of Jerusalem"* here on earth at the close of the Tribulation period. In a later chapter of this book we will learn that Jesus will come to establish His earthly kingdom and that there will be those who will yet be alive and enter into that kingdom. I believe that these 144,000 are only a few of the many that will be alive at the time Jesus establishes His kingdom on earth. At no time in Revelation do we see that the 144,000 are killed. We do not find any place where it says that they are resurrected. Therefore, they **must still** be alive, and living on the earth. Thus Mount Zion would have to refer to the Mount of Olives, which is east of Jerusalem.

John hears a sound *"from heaven"* that he says *"was like that of harpists playing their harps. And they sang a new song before the four living creatures and the elders. No one could learn the song except the 144,000 who had been redeemed from the earth."* Many try to say that because of what is said here the 144,000 are in heaven and have been resurrected. However, this is **not** the meaning of the verse. The fact that the *"harpists"* are playing a new song in the presence of *"the four living creatures and the elders"* indicates that they are in heaven and that it is possibly the martyred saints who perhaps attempt to learn this new song. However, the 144,000 are with Jesus on the earth. They hear the new song and we are told that only they are able to learn the song. Jesus and the 144,000 are on the earth, but they still are able to hear the *"new song"* and learn it. Because they have been sealed by the angels with the seal of God, as seen in Revelation chapter seven, they are thus *"redeemed from the earth."* They have not defiled their lives with wickedness and *"no lie was found in their mouths."* John F. Walvoord, author of The Revelation Of Jesus Christ, states the following: *"If the 144,000 are on earth in Zion, who then are the company in heaven? Though the natural questions concerning their identity are not clearly answered in the text, the heavenly group are probably the martyred saints of the tribulation, in contrast to the 144,000 who are on earth and do not suffer martyrdom. Both groups, however, experience the trials of the great tribulation and therefore are alone worthy to enter into the song of redemption recounting their victory over their enemies and praising God for His grace which has numbered them among the redeemed."* (Used by permission from Moody Publishers, Copyright, 1966.)

In summary, the 144,000 who were sealed with the *"seal of the living God"* (Rev. 7:2) are seen at the close of the Tribulation period, standing with Jesus in victory! They have survived the trials and the sufferings during the last three and one half years of the Tribulation period. They are the *"firstfruits"* that are offered to God and to the Lamb. They will enter into the

Millennial Kingdom, Christ's earthly kingdom, and will live with Him for a thousand years!

1. Vision Of The Angel With The Everlasting Gospel

"Then I saw another angel flying in midair, and he had the eternal gospel to proclaim to those who live on the earth—to every nation, tribe, language and people. He said in a loud voice, 'Fear God and give him glory, because the hour of his judgment has come. Worship him who made the heavens, the earth, the sea and the springs of water.'" (Rev. 14:6-7 NIV)

Here we are told that John sees *"another angel flying in midair, and he had the eternal gospel."* The King James Version says it is *"the everlasting gospel."* It would seem that the everlasting gospel would be the gospel of God's righteousness in judgment rather than the gospel of His grace or salvation. We are told that the angel says *"Fear God and give him glory, because the hour of his judgment has come."* God is about to deal with the wickedness of mankind and in so doing He will establish His sovereignty over the entire world. Those who are on the earth and have decided to live for God are told to give God glory and to *"worship him who made the heavens, the earth, the sea and the springs of water."*

2. Babylon's Fall Foretold

"A second angel followed and said, 'Fallen! Fallen is Babylon the Great, which made all the nations drink the maddening wine of her adulteries.'" (Rev. 14:8 NIV)

As stated earlier, after the seventh bowl judgment another parenthetical section will be discussed. This parenthetical section will be about Babylon. Here, we are given the vision of the prediction of Babylon's fall. In prophecy, Babylon is often called the literal city, sometimes a political system and sometimes referred to as a religious system. However, since this vision is about the end of the Tribulation period and the beginning of the Millennial period, it would seem that this prophecy of Babylon is to be understood as the literal city. (This subject will be discussed in more detail later in this study.)

3. Followers Of Antichrist To Be Doomed

"A third angel followed them and said in a loud voice: ' If anyone worships the beast and his image and receives his mark on their forehead or on the hand, he, too, will drink of the wine of God's fury, which has been poured full strength into the cup of his wrath. He will be tormented with burning sulphur in the presence of the holy angels and of the Lamb. And the smoke of their torment rises for ever and ever. There is no rest day or night for those who worship the beast and his image, or for anyone who receives the mark of his name.' This calls for patient endurance on the part of the saints who obey God's commandments and remain faithful to Jesus." (Rev. 14:9-12 NIV)

Here the third angel says, *"If anyone worships the beast and his image and receives his mark...he, too, will drink of the wine of God's fury."* If the people who are living on the earth during the Great Tribulation allow themselves to receive the mark of the beast and worship him, they will be doomed eternally. These verses are self explanatory, in that those who follow after the *"beast"* will be *"tormented with burning sulphur."* They will not only endure the plagues and torments of the judgments that are to be poured out upon evil mankind during this period, but they will end up in the lake of fire for all eternity. (Rev. 19:20) They will have *"no rest day or night."* Those who will live for the Lord during this time are told that they must endure patiently. Soon the *"KING OF KINGS AND LORD OF LORDS"* (Rev. 19:16) will come and put an end to all the evil in the earth.

4. Blessedness Of The Holy Dead

"Then I heard a voice from heaven say, 'Write: Blessed are the dead who die in the Lord from now on.' 'Yes,' says the Spirit, 'they will rest from their labor, for their deeds will follow them.'" (Rev. 14:13 NIV)

John hears a voice in heaven pronounce a blessing upon those who *"die in the Lord from now on."* This is not to say that those who have died previously are not blessed, for surely they are. Rather, these who die during this particular time, during the last half of the Tribulation period, will be those who are martyred for their faith in Jesus. It is these who we are told *"will rest from their labor"* and *"their deeds will follow them."* These are the saints that have been instructed in the previous verse that they must have *"patient endurance."*

5. Vision Of Armageddon

"I looked, and there before me was a white cloud, and seated on the cloud was one 'like a son of man' with a crown of gold on his head and a sharp sickle in his hand. Then another angel came out of the temple and called in a loud voice to him who was sitting on the cloud, 'Take your sickle and reap, because the time to reap has come, for the harvest of the earth is ripe.' So he who was seated on the cloud swung his sickle over the earth, and the earth was harvested. Another angel came out of the temple in heaven, and he too had a sharp sickle. Still another angel, who had charge of the fire, came from the altar and called in a loud voice to him who had the sharp sickle, 'Take your sharp sickle and gather the clusters of grapes from the earth's vine, because its grapes are ripe.' The angel swung his sickle on the earth, gathered its grapes and threw them into the great winepress of God's wrath. They were trampled in the winepress outside the city, and blood flowed out of the press, rising as high as the horses' bridles for the distance of 1,600 stadia." (Rev. 14: 14-20 NIV)

John now sees a vision of the end of the Tribulation period, which closes with the Second Coming of Jesus to the earth. The end of the Tribulation period climaxes with both the Second Coming of Christ and the battle of Armageddon. It will be at this time when Antichrist will have brought all of his armies and those who are allied with him into Israel and they will surround Jerusalem to do battle. The intent of this battle is to destroy Jerusalem and the Jews who have not yielded to the demands of Antichrist. The two witnesses that were spoken of earlier will suddenly come to life and will be resurrected before the eyes of those watching. Suddenly, Jesus will arrive on the scene. Here we are told that one *"like a son of man"* who has upon his head a crown of gold and a sharp sickle in his hand is *"seated"* on a white cloud. Later in Revelation, at the time of Jesus' Second Coming, we are told that He will be riding a *"white horse."* (Rev. 19:11) This is not to say that there is any contradiction. The fact that He is said to be seated on a white cloud in the above verses is not to say that He will not ride a white horse also. Jesus could very well ride the white horse and then seat Himself upon the white cloud to carry out the harvesting of the earth as here in these verses.

We are told that another angel comes forth and says to the one seated on the white cloud, *"Take your sickle and reap, because the time to reap has come, for the harvest of the earth is ripe."* It would seem that this is a message to begin the judgment of the wicked on the earth. The *"harvest"* here referred to is indicative of that of dried and withered fruit. Thus the rotten and immoral souls of mankind are now being dealt with by the use of the *"sharp sickle."*

There are those who believe that the *"harvest"* referred to in verses 15 and 16 is a reference to the resurrection of the saints, whereas the *"harvest"* referred to in verses 18-20 is a reference to the resurrection of the wicked to eternal damnation. However, this understanding cannot be the true meaning of these verses, since there will be many of the saints left to live on the earth during the following Millennial period. The martyred saints and those who die for their refusal to take the mark of the *"beast"* will be resurrected, but this *"harvest"* does not refer to them. (See Rev. 20: 4) The wicked are here being harvested and not the saints. The fact that the wicked are the ones being harvested is not to say that they are being resurrected. Here the wicked are slain and done away with. They will be resurrected later at the close of the Millennial period. (See Rev. 20:5)

All of the above verses are in reference to the coming war between Antichrist and Christ at Armageddon. (See Rev. 19:17-21) Antichrist and all of his followers will be slain. Not one will escape this judgment. Only those who have not yielded to the demands of Antichrist will survive this war. All who have received the mark of the *"beast"* and who worship him and his image will be slain in this battle. We are told that *"blood flowed out of the press, rising as high as the horses' bridles for a distance of 1600 stadia."* Many people think that the blood of mankind will actually flow as high as a horse's bridle. However, it is better to understand that the bloodletting of this time will actually mean that the blood would splatter as high as the horse's bridles. The *"distance of 1600 stadia"* is actually about 180 miles, or 300 kilometers, according to the NIV Bible reference. Others say it is approximately 200 miles. Either case would be an excessive amount of space. However, one should interpret this to be the actual distance, for the armies of the world will be gathered here. Thus, it would most likely take all of the area to be able to hold them all. Jerusalem will be totally surrounded by the armies of Antichrist. One would think that Jerusalem is about to be doomed. But it will be Antichrist and his armies that will be doomed. As stated earlier, not one of Antichrist's followers will escape judgment.

3. The Seventh Trumpet Judgment

We now come back to the chronological events of the Tribulation period. All of the events that have been discussed between the sixth trumpet judgment and the seventh trumpet judgment have been parenthetical events. As has been stated many times, these events do not advance the narrative of the book of Revelation, rather they add to the overall picture and help us to understand the book better.

The seventh seal judgment contains the seven trumpet judgments. We are now at the seventh trumpet judgment, which contains the seven last plagues, or seven bowl judgments. However, the seventh seal judgment is all inclusive of all the trumpet and bowl judgments. The chronological order of events then would be, (1) the opening of the seven seal judgments in which the seven trumpet judgments are included in the seventh seal, (2) the sounding of the seven trumpet judgments in which the seven bowl judgments are included in the seventh trumpet judgment and (3) the pouring out of the seven bowl judgments. The Tribulation period comes to its climax at the end of the seventh bowl judgment, at which time Jesus returns to the earth at His Second Coming, which is also the time when Antichrist gathers all the armies of the world to Armageddon.

1. The Second *"Woe"* Is Past—The Third *"Woe"* Comes Quickly

"The second woe is past and behold, the third woe cometh quickly." (Rev. 11:14)

The events that took place during the fifth trumpet judgment was the first *"woe."* The second *"woe"* was the events that were in the sixth trumpet judgment. We are now told that *"the third woe cometh quickly."* As stated above, the events of the seventh trumpet judgment includes the seven bowl judgments. All of the terrible judgments that will come upon mankind who dwell on the earth will make up this final *"woe."*

a. Christ's Reign Foreseen

"And the seventh angel sounded; and there were great voices in heaven, saying, the kingdom of this world is become the kingdom of our Lord, and of his Christ, and he shall reign forever and ever. And the four and twenty elders, who sat before God on their thrones, fell upon their faces, and worshipped God, Saying, We give thee thanks, O Lord God Almighty, who art, and wast, and art to come, because thou hast taken to thee thy great power, and hast reigned. And the nations were angry, and thy wrath is come, and the time of the dead, that they should be judged, and that thou shouldest give reward unto thy servants, the prophets, and to the saints, and them that fear thy name, small and great, and shouldest destroy them who destroy the earth. And the temple of God was opened in heaven, and there was seen in his temple the ark of his covenant; and there were lightnings, and voices, and thunderclaps, and an earthquake, and great hail." (Rev. 11:15-19)

John hears the seventh angel sound the trumpet, and he sees a vision of the kingdoms of the world becoming *"the kingdom of our Lord and his Christ."* One would wonder how this could be seeing that the seven bowl judgments have not yet been poured out. The answer is, however, as stated earlier, that the seven bowl judgments are included in the seventh trumpet judgment. This is at the close of the Seventieth week, or the Tribulation period. Once Jesus destroys the wicked, and Antichrist and his false prophet are cast into the lake of fire, (Rev. 19:20) He will become the Ruler of the kingdoms of the earth. (See Zech. 14:9-11)

We are told that Christ's reign will be *"forever and ever."* Although we understand that the Millennial period will last for only one thousand years in which Christ will be the King, we must also understand that His Kingship will continue in the New Heaven and New Earth. Never again will man be subject to the sinful rule of other men or by Satan.

We are told the twenty four elders *"fell upon their faces, and worshipped God, Saying, We give thee thanks, O Lord God Almighty, who art, and wast, and art to come..."* The fact that God is referred to in this statement that He is and was and is to come is indicative that He has always existed and will continue to exist forever. We understand that He has no beginning and no ending of days. He is always omnipresent and will be forever.

In verse 18 we are told the *"nations were angry, and thy wrath has come."* The fact that God is pouring out His great wrath upon the earth and the wicked therein, angers the people and they are slain in their anger. God's wrath is holy whereas the anger of sinful man is sin. We are further told that *"the time of the dead, that they should be judged, and that thou shouldest give reward unto thy servants, the prophets, and to the saints, and them that fear thy name, small and great, and shouldest destroy them who destroy the earth."* This is in reference to the resurrection of the saints that died during the Tribulation period. The *"prophets"* could very well be in reference to the two witnesses, whereas it will be at the close of the Tribulation period when they will be resurrected. All those *"that fear"* the name of God, in other words, those who chose to serve God rather than take the mark of the *"beast"* and who died because of their testimony will also be resurrected at this time. As stated before, all of this is consummated at the close of the Tribulation period, which is when the seventh trumpet judgment is sounded, and the seven bowl judgments are poured out. At His coming to the earth, Jesus will destroy those who have defiled the earth with their sinful ways.

In verse 19, John says that *"the temple of God was opened in heaven."* When it was opened, we are told that there are lightnings, voices, and thunderings, and on the earth there was an earthquake and great hail. Although this is a scene of the temple in heaven, the aftermath of it being opened overflows into the earth with an *"earthquake, and great hail."* It would seem that this is the dramatic climax of God's wrath on the earth and bringing the Tribulation period to its close. Therefore, the stage is now set for the pouring out of each of the bowl judgments upon the earth and those that dwell therein.

b. The Seven Bowl Judgments

"And I saw another sign in heaven, great and marvelous, seven angels having the seven last plagues; for in them is filled up the wrath of God. And I saw, as it were, a sea of glass mingled with fire, and them that had gotten the victory over the beast, and over his image, and over his mark, and over the number of his name, standing on the sea of glass, having the harps of God. And they sing the song of Moses, the servant of God, and the song of the Lamb, saying, Great and marvelous are thy works, Lord God Almighty; just and true are thy ways, thou King of saints. Who shall not fear thee, O Lord, and glorify thy name? For thou only art holy; for all nations shall come and worship before thee; for thy judgments are made manifest. And after that I looked and, behold, the temple of the tabernacle of the testimony in heaven was opened. And the seven angels came out of the temple, having the seven plagues, clothed in pure and white linen, and having their breasts girded with golden girdles. And one of the four living creatures gave unto the seven angels seven golden bowls full of the wrath of God, who liveth forever and ever. And the temple was filled with smoke from the glory of God, and from his power; and no man was able to enter into the temple till the seven plagues of the seven angels were fulfilled." (Rev. 15:1-8)

As has been stated earlier, the chronological order of events during the last half of the Tribulation period are all within the seven seal judgments. The seventh seal judgment includes all of the seven trumpet judgments and the seven bowl judgments. Immediately after the seven bowl judgments are poured out, the chronological order of events continues in Revelation, chapter 19. Chapters 17 and 18 of Revelation are another interlude or parenthetical section of the book, which will be discussed a little later.

John tells us that he sees *"another sign in heaven"* Thus the vision he now sees introduces to us the *"seven angels having the seven last plagues."* These seven angels are a different group of angels from those that had the seven trumpets. We are told that they have the *"seven last plagues,"* meaning that all of the other judgments were also plagues in that they were divine judgments of God's wrath. These are the last of the judgments of God's wrath to be poured out upon the earth and those that dwell therein. After these seven bowl judgments, Jesus comes to the earth to establish His earthly kingdom. The battle of Armageddon, which will be discussed a little later, will be fought and Jesus will become the ultimate victor.

John states that he saw *"as it were, a sea of glass mingled with fire."* In Rev. 4:6 he said that he had seen *"a sea of glass like crystal."* Both are in the midst of the throne of God. The heavenly hosts are said to be *"standing on the sea of glass"* thereby eliminating the idea that it is a natural sea. It would seem that this sea of glass represents God's glory and that He is able to sustain those in His presence with His power. All of those who have *"gotten the victory over the beast, and over his image, and over his mark, and over the number of his name"* are the martyred saints who were killed by the *"beast."* Although they were killed for their testimony of Christ, they have won the victory over the evil of the world and the *"beast."*

The martyred saints are said to *"sing the song of Moses, the servant of God, and the song of the Lamb."* They ascribe praise to

God by saying, *"Great and marvelous are thy works, Lord God Almighty; just and true are thy ways, thou King of the saints."* These have given their lives in defense of God's Word and they now are able to reap the benefits because God's Word is true.

The question is asked, *"Who shall not fear thee, O Lord and glorify thy name?"* Although most of those that dwell upon the earth are evil and have no love or regard for God, they will soon be forced to acknowledge Him. They will someday stand before God to give an account of what they had done while living on the earth. They will know that they have made the wrong choice and they will be cast into the lake of fire for all eternity because of that choice. However, the time will be coming soon when all nations and people of the earth will acknowledge God and they will worship Him. We are told, *"for all nations shall come and worship before thee."* Others foretold this in the Bible. (See Dan. 7:14; Zeph. 2:11; Zech. 14:9)

The remaining verses of chapter 15 give us the picture of the preparation of the seven angels who are to pour out the last plagues upon the earth and upon evil mankind. We are told that the *"seven angels came out of the temple, having the seven plagues, clothed in pure and white linen, and having their breasts girded with golden girdles."* I stated earlier that, after the saints of God stand before the Judgment Seat of Christ, they will be *"arrayed in fine linen, clean and white."* (Rev. 19:8) We are told that the fine linen represents the righteousness of God. Therefore, the *"pure and white linen"* would seem to represent the righteousness of the judgments that the seven angels are about to pour out. God's judgments upon the earth and the wicked that dwell therein are righteous judgments. God's wrath is justified and is only against the vile and wickedness of those upon the earth. The glory of God will endure and He will receive righteous glory and praise from those who fear Him and serve Him.

1. The First Bowl Judgment

"And I heard a great voice out of the temple saying to the seven angels, Go your ways, and pour out the bowls of the wrath of God upon the earth. And the first went, and poured out his bowl upon the earth, and there fell a foul and painful sore upon the men who had the mark of the beast, and upon them who worship his image." (Rev. 16:1-2)

The command is given to the seven angels who have the seven last plagues to *"Go your ways, and pour out the bowls of the wrath of God upon the earth."* We are then told that the first of these angels *"poured out his bowl upon the earth, and there fell a foul and painful sore upon the men who had the mark of the beast, and upon them who worship his image."* In the first trumpet judgment, a third part of the trees and all the green grass were affected. Here the judgment is upon the people of the earth. However, **only** those who *"had the mark of the beast"* and those who *"worship his image"* are affected. We are told that *"there fell a foul and painful sore"* upon these people. This *"sore"* would seem to be similar to that of the boils that the Egyptians had sustained during the time when Moses was trying to get Pharaoh to agree to let the Israelites leave Egypt. (Ex. 9:9-11) Only those that refuse to take the mark of the beast or worship his image are spared this terrible *"sore."* This event takes place during the last part of the Tribulation period because we are told that only those *"who had the mark of the beast"* and those *"who worship his image"* are affected.

2. The Second Bowl Judgment

"And the second angel poured out his bowl upon the sea, and it became like the blood of a dead man; and every living soul died in the sea." (Rev. 16:3)

During the second trumpet judgment, we are told that a third of the sea was affected by the judgment. Here, it seems that this judgment spreads to all of the seas. We are told that the seas become *"like the blood of a dead man."* It is more likely that the seas take the appearance of blood, but that the chemical in the waters has now been changed and that *"every living soul"* dies. Every creature in the sea dies, which would cause a terrible shortage of food for those that live on the earth. Since a major portion of the earth is embodied with water, this judgment would then affect all of this area.

3. The Third Bowl Judgment

"And the third angel poured out his bowl upon the rivers and fountains of waters, and they became blood. And I heard the angel of the waters say, Thou art righteous, O Lord, who art, and wast, and shalt be, because thou hast judged thus. For they have shed the blood of saints and prophets, and thou hast given them blood to drink; for they are worthy. And I heard another out of the altar say, Even so, Lord God Almighty, true and righteous are thy judgments." (Rev. 16:4-7)

As in the third trumpet judgment, the waters are turned to blood. However, in the third trumpet judgment a third of the rivers and fountains of waters are affected. Here, the judgment extends to all of the rivers and fountains of waters throughout the earth. As stated in the third trumpet judgment, there is no reason to not accept these rivers and fountains of waters to be literal. All of the waters of the rivers and fountains of waters are turned to blood. Thus it would seem that the same result of death would come to the creatures in the rivers just as was so of those in the seas, although we are not told this.

We are told that the *"angel of the waters"* justifies this judgment because the wicked of the earth have shed the blood of the saints and the prophets. He says that they are worthy to drink the blood. Then someone else from *"the altar"* agrees and says, *"Even so, Lord God Almighty, true and righteous are thy judgments."* It now seems that all of the seas of the world and all the rivers and fountains of water throughout the world have been judged and their waters have been turned to blood. God has judged and the blood of the saints who have been martyred has now been vindicated.

4. The Fourth Bowl Judgment

"And the fourth angel poured out his bowl upon the sun, and power was given unto him to scorch men with fire. And men were scorched with great heat, and blasphemed the name of God, who hath power over these plagues; and they repented not to give him glory." (Rev. 16:8-9)

The fourth bowl judgment stands in contrast to the fourth trumpet judgment, in that, in the fourth trumpet judgment, a third of the sun, moon and stars are affected so that the light would decrease upon the earth. In this judgment, the bowl is poured out only on the sun, and the angel is given the power to cause the sun to increase in heat to scorch the wicked people on the earth. We are told that these people will be scorched with great heat and fire and they still do not repent. They continue to *"blaspheme the name of God."* It will only be those that have received the mark of the beast and who worship the image of the beast who will be affected by the fire with which the angel has power to scorch men by the sun. We are not told how the saints who are still alive on the earth are protected, but they will not be affected by the sun's heat. God allows this judgment to come **only** upon the wicked.

5. The Fifth Bowl Judgment

"And the fifth angel poured out his bowl upon the throne of the beast, and his kingdom was full of darkness; and they gnawed their tongues for pain, And blasphemed the God of heaven because of their pains and their sores, and repented not of their deeds." (Rev. 16:10-11)

Here we are told that the angel pours out his bowl *"upon the throne of the beast, and his kingdom was full of darkness; and they gnawed their tongues for pain."* This is the throne of Antichrist that the bowl is poured out upon. The result is darkness upon his kingdom. Because of the burns and the sores from the fire of the sun that they have sustained by the previous judgments, the unrepentant suffer tremendous pain. They evidently recognize that these judgments are a result of their wicked ways and that the judgments come from God, yet they do not repent. They continue to *"blaspheme the God of heaven because of their pains and their sores."* We are told that *"they gnawed their tongues for pain."* This is a description of tremendous and terrible pain.

6. The Sixth Bowl Judgment

"And the sixth angel poured out his bowl upon the great river, Euphrates, and its water was dried up, that the way of the kings of the east might be prepared." (Rev. 16:12)

When the sixth trumpet was sounded, we found the *"four angels"* who had been bound at the river Euphrates were loosed. The Euphrates River is the eastern boundary of the land that was promised to Abraham and his people. (See Gen. 15:18; Deut. 1:7; 11:24; Josh. 1:4) It is also the eastern boundary of the old Roman Empire. Here the angel pours out his bowl upon the Euphrates River and the result is that it dries up so *"that the way of the kings of the east might be prepared. "* Therefore, the way is now prepared for the invasion of the eastern kingdoms to join with the kingdom of the north to come against Antichrist and eventually fight against Jesus at His Second Coming. The war that Antichrist fights against the kings out of the east and out of the north (Dan. 11:44) will result in Antichrist gaining victory over them, and their armies will then join with him in fighting Jesus at Armageddon.

7. The Seventh Bowl Judgment

Between the sixth and seventh seal judgments and the sixth and seventh trumpet judgments there was an interlude or parenthetical span of time. The same is here between the sixth and seventh bowl judgments, in verses 13 through 16. This interlude concerns the battle of Armageddon. This will be discussed a little later.

"And the seventh angel poured out his bowl into the air, and there came a great voice out of the temple of heaven, from the throne, saying, It is done. And there were voices, and thunders, and lightnings; and there was a great earthquake, such as was not since men were upon the earth, so mighty an earthquake, and so great. And the great city was divided into three parts, and the cities of the nations fell; and great Babylon came in remembrance before God, to give unto her the cup of the wine of the fierceness of his wrath. And every island fled away, and the mountains were not found. And there fell upon men a great hail out of heaven, every stone about the weight of a talent; and men blasphemed God because of the plague of the hail; for the plague was exceedingly great." (Rev. 16:17-21)

The time of this judgment is just prior to the Second Coming of Jesus. The only event to take place prior to Jesus' return to the earth is the gathering of all the armies of the earth together at Armageddon, which will be discussed a little later. We are told that the seventh angel pours out his bowl *"into the air,"* signifying greater havoc on the earth and upon mankind than before. Once the bowl is poured into the air, we are told that *"there came a great voice out of the temple of heaven, from the throne, saying, It is done."* We are not told who speaks here. Could it be God Himself? Jesus, when He died on the cross said, *"It is finished."* (St. John 19:30)

In the next verse we are told that *"there were voices, and thunders, and lightnings; and there was a great earthquake such as was not since men were upon the earth, so mighty an earthquake, and so great."* When the final seal and trumpet judgments were unleashed there were voices, thunderings, lightnings and earthquakes. However, here the earthquake is said to be greater than any previous earthquake, *"such as was not since men were upon the earth."* This seems to be picturesque of the earth in literal upheaval as a result of the judgment that is poured out.

The *"great city"* is said to become divided into three parts. There are some differing opinions as to what city is represented here. Some say it is Babylon, while others say it is Jerusalem. It was earlier determined that Jerusalem is the *"great city, which is spiritually called Sodom and Egypt, where also our Lord was crucified."* (Rev. 11:8) We are told in St. Matt. 24:15 that Antichrist will *"stand in the holy place,"* which is in the Temple of the Jews in Jerusalem. Therefore, it seems that Antichrist will set up his headquarters in Jerusalem, thereby making Jerusalem the *"great city,"* which is referred to as Babylon **only** because Antichrist operates his kingdom from here. The fact that it is said to be divided into three parts indicates that it is not totally destroyed. We are further told that the *"cities of the nations fell."* This implies that the great earthquake is to be felt throughout the world. Every island and *"the mountains"* will disappear; indicating the catastrophe will be worldwide. Therefore, the terrain of the world will experience total change.

We are told that *"Babylon came in remembrance before God, to give unto her the cup of the wine of the fierceness of his wrath."* In verse 21 we are told that *"there fell upon men a great hail out of heaven, and every stone about the weight of a talent."* A *"talent"* is considered to be approximately 100 pounds. There have been differences among some people as to the actual meaning of the weight of the *"talent."* Some say it is actually 90 pounds, while others say it is between 90 and 100 pounds. The fact of the matter is, whether the actual weight is 90 or 100 pounds, when these stones come down out of heaven and hit the earth they will devastate whatever is still standing after the earthquake! A man will not be able to determine if the weight is 90 or 100 pounds if these stones hit him, for either will utterly destroy him. Some scholars have suggested that the *"great hail"* could possibly refer to bombs that are dropped from aircraft. However, it is preferable to accept the *"great hail"* to be literally large stones of hail hurled down from heaven as a judgment of God upon the wicked.

Still the people will not repent and turn from their evil ways. We are told that they will continue to blaspheme God *"because of the plague of the hail; for the plague was exceedingly great."* Although one would think that with all the plagues that have been issued upon mankind, people would repent and change their way of living. But they continue in their sins and continue to blaspheme God for their fate.

This judgment comes just prior to the Second Coming of Christ. As stated earlier, only one event yet remains to be fulfilled prior to Jesus' coming to the earth, which is the gathering of the armies of the world to Armageddon. This event will be discussed very soon. But first, the interlude, or parenthetical event of Revelation, chapters 17 and 18, will be discussed.

4. Interlude: The Doom Of Babylon

Prior to discussing the parenthetical event that comes between the sixth and seventh bowl judgments, the interlude or parenthetical event of Revelation 17 and 18 needs to be discussed. This interlude deals with Babylon in its religious and political forms. Babylon is actually the seat of Antichrist who rules over the Revived Grecian Empire and the Revised Roman Empire. It will be destroyed along with the other cities of the earth in the seventh bowl judgment. As stated earlier, Babylon is possibly another name for the kingdom or the city in which Antichrist rules.

1. Babylon's Fall Foretold

"And there followed another angel, saying, Babylon is fallen, is fallen, that great city, because she made all nations drink of the wine of the wrath of her fornication." (Rev. 14:8)

As stated earlier, Babylon is sometimes referred to in prophecy as a literal city, sometimes to a religious system or sometimes to a political system. It would seem that in this prophecy, Babylon is another name for the kingdom of Antichrist. Babylon will fall at the time of the seventh bowl judgment, due mostly because of the great earthquake that was previously mentioned. However, God will issue a specific judgment upon Babylon, as mentioned in Rev. 16:19, where we are told that He will give to Babylon *"the cup of the wine of the fierceness of his wrath."* Here, we are told that *"Babylon is fallen, is fallen."* The repetitious statement, *"is fallen,"* is basically there to emphasize the fact that Babylon **will** fall. Because Babylon has caused many to *"drink of the wine of the wrath of her fornication,"* God will deal with her mightily and she will no longer exist.

a. The Harlot: The Apostate Church

"And there came one of the seven angels who had the seven bowls, and talked with me, saying unto me, Come here; I will show unto thee the judgment of the great harlot that sitteth upon many waters; With whom the kings of the earth have committed fornication, and the inhabitants of the earth have been made drunk with the wine of her fornication. So he carried me away in the Spirit into the wilderness and I saw a woman sit upon a scarlet colored beast, full of the names of blasphemy, having seven heads and ten horns. And the woman was arrayed in purple and scarlet color, and bedecked with gold and precious stones and pearls, having a golden cup in her hand, full of abominations and filthiness of her fornication; And upon her forehead was a name written, MYSTERY, BABYLON THE GREAT, THE MOTHER OF HARLOTS AND ABOMINA-TIONS OF THE EARTH. And I saw the woman drunk with the blood of the saints, and with the blood of the martyrs of Jesus; and when I saw her, I wondered with great wonder." (Rev. 17:1-6)

The events of Revelation 17 and 18 are parenthetical to the normal flow of the events of the Tribulation period. Revelation 17 deals with Babylon in its religious form, whereas chapter 18 deals with Babylon in its political form. The events in chapter 17 most likely occur at the beginning of the Great Tribulation, which is at the beginning of the last half of the Tribulation period. As stated earlier, Babylon is perhaps another name for the kingdom of Antichrist, or the beast of Revelation 13. Some teachers believe that Babylon is actually a literal city. Because of the fact that we are told that the beast upon which the *"woman"* sits is said to have *"seven heads and ten horns,"* many believe that this literal city is Rome.

We are told that John sees a *"woman"* who is sitting *"upon a scarlet colored beast."* This beast is said to have *"seven heads and ten horns."* This is the description of the beast of Revelation 13, who also has seven heads and ten horns. Therefore, it is a picture of the same beast. As we know, Rome was literally built upon seven mountains, and was known as the "City of Seven Hills." When the old Roman Empire becomes the Revised Roman Empire, it will have ten kings over ten kingdoms. However, as we have seen, one of the kings of one of the ten kingdoms rises up and wages war against three of the kingdoms within the Revised Roman Empire and will *"subdue"* them. (Dan. 7:24) This will bring about the Revived Grecian Empire, over which Antichrist becomes the ruler. Therefore, the *"beast"* upon which the woman sits is none other than the Revised Roman Empire, of which the Revived Grecian Empire is included.

But who is the *"woman"* or the *"harlot"* in these verses? She is actually known as Apostate Christendom, which is headed up by the false prophet. We are told that the *"great harlot"* sits upon *"many waters."* The *"waters"* in this verse refers to people and nations. Therefore, it is the nations of people that the false religion of the Apostate Church is spoken of here and is headed up by the false prophet. The fact that the *"woman"* is said to be *"arrayed in purple and scarlet color, and bedecked with gold and precious stones and pearls, having a golden cup in her hand, full of abominations and filthiness of her fornication;"* is indicative of the leadership of the false prophet over the Apostate Church. This is a picture of the false prophet being robed in all the religious glamour and pomp of a false religion. This false religion is spread worldwide and the people throughout the world are seduced into believing all the lies of the false prophet and Antichrist. Because Rome is the home of the Vatican and the Pope of the Catholic Religion, many believe that it will be Roman Catholicism that will be the Apostate religion headed up by the Pope, who they believe to be the false prophet. Whoever the false prophet will be is not yet known. However, he will be the leader of the false religion and he will be seated in power with Antichrist.

We are told that upon the forehead of the *"harlot,"* a name was written. The name is *"BABYLON THE GREAT, THE MOTHER OF HARLOTS AND ABOMINATIONS OF THE EARTH."* The word *"MYSTERY"* actually is not part of the title or name. It is believed that when John saw this vision, it was such an astonishing one of mystery. Possibly those who interpreted the Bible misunderstood and included the word as part of the name. At any rate, the name is self explanatory, in that, this false religion is the mother of idolatry and perversions, which are abominations unto God.

The woman is said to be *"drunk with the blood of the saints, and the blood of the martyrs of Jesus."* The false prophet will head up the false religion of the Apostate Church and they will be responsible for the cause of death to many of the saints and those martyred. They will think they are doing what is right in the sight of God by killing the true saints of God. But they are deceived and blindly follow after the *"beast."* The Apostate religion will be the persecutors of the saints during the Tribulation period. To John, this is so appalling that he says that he *"wondered with great wonder."*

b. The Harlot And The Beast

"And the angel said unto me, Why didst thou wonder? I will tell thee the mystery of the woman, and of the beast that carrieth her, which hath the seven heads and ten horns. The beast that thou sawest was, and is not, and shall ascend out of the bottomless pit, and go into perdition; and they that dwell on the earth shall wonder, whose names were not written in the book of life from the foundation of the world, when they behold the beast that was, and is not, and yet is. And here is the mind which hath wisdom. The seven heads are seven mountains, on which the woman sitteth. And there are seven kings: five are fallen, and one is, and the other is not yet come; and when he cometh, he must continue a short space. And the beast that was, and is not, even he is the eighth, and is of the seven, and goeth into perdition. And the ten horns which thou sawest are ten kings, who

have received no kingdom as yet, but receive power as kings one hour with the beast. These have one mind, and shall give their power and strength unto the beast." (Rev. 17:7-13)

In verse seven, the angel asks John, *"Why didst thou wonder?"* But John was so astonished by what he had seen that he possibly could not help himself. The angel goes on to tell him that he would explain to him about the *"mystery of the woman, and of the beast that carrieth her."* In doing so, the angel explains the mystery of the beast first, then the woman second.

"The beast that thou sawest was, and is not, and shall ascend out of the bottomless pit, and goeth into perdition..." This statement has brought about a lot of confusion on the part of many scholars of Revelation. The beast spoken of here refers to the world power or political entity of the Revised Roman Empire, of which the Revived Grecian Empire is included. The Revived Grecian Empire is the *"beast that was,"* and at the time of this vision which John is seeing, it *"is not,"* meaning that it is seemingly dead. When the Grecian Empire becomes revived, it will be as though the *"deadly wound was healed."* (Rev. 13:3) However, the beast that rises or ascends *"out of the bottomless pit"* is Satan. Satan is the ruler of the bottomless pit and it is he that will ascend from this pit to impose his power upon the one who rules over the Revived Grecian Empire, i.e. Antichrist. In his book entitled The Revelation Of Jesus Christ, John F. Walvoord says, *"There is a confusing similarity between the descriptions afforded Satan who was apparently described as the king over the demons in the abyss (9:11), "the beast that ascendeth out of the bottomless pit" (11:7), the beast whose "deadly wound was healed" (13:3), and the beast of 17:8. The solution to this intricate problem is that there is an identification to some extent of Satan with the future world ruler and identification of the world ruler with his world government. Each of the three entities is described as a beast. Only Satan himself actually comes from the abyss. The world*

government which he promotes is entirely satanic in its power and to this extent is identified with Satan. It is the beast as the world government which is revived. The man who is the world ruler, however, has power and great authority given to him by Satan. The fact that Satan and the world ruler are referred to in similar terms indicates their close relationship one to the other.

While many have attempted to demonstrate from this verse that the final world ruler is some resurrected being such as Judas Iscariot, Nero, or one of the more recent world rulers, it would seem preferable to regard the "eighth" beast as the political power of the world government rather than its human ruler. What is revived is imperial government, not an imperial ruler (cf. Rev. 13:3). That which seemingly went out of existence in history never to be revived is thus miraculously resuscitated at the end of the age." (Used by permission from Moody Publishers, Copyright, 1966) Therefore, it will be the Revived Grecian Empire that will be the satanic seat of Antichrist and Satan will give power and great authority to the ruler of the *"beast,"* which is the empire itself. The reference to this beast as being a world government and the one who rules over this empire as a world ruler should be understood that the government is a world government in the same way as the government of the United States as being a world government. Therefore, the term given to the ruler of the Revived Grecian Empire as a world ruler would be in the same way as the President of the United States is recognized as a world ruler or leader.

When the Revived Grecian Empire comes into existence the people that *"dwell on the earth shall wonder"* (vs.8) *"after the beast."* (Rev. 13:3) These who will be taken up or engulfed in amazement concerning this beast are those *"whose names were not written in the book of life from the foundation of the world."* They are those who have rejected God and who oppose Him.

The angel continues to tell John, *"here is the mind which hath wisdom. The seven heads are seven mountains, on which the woman sitteth."* This is in reference to Rome, which, as stated earlier, was built on seven hills. Then the angel says, *"there are seven kings: five are fallen, and one is, and the other is not yet come; and when he cometh, he must continue a short space. And the beast that was, and is not, even he is the eighth, and is of the seven, and goeth into perdition."* Of the *"seven kings"* we are told that *"five are fallen."* I mentioned earlier that these five were Egypt, Assyria, Babylon, Medo-Persia and Greece. These five kingdoms no longer exist at the time of this vision. We are told that *"one is"* and it is in reference to the old Roman Empire, which was in power at the time of this vision. *"The other is not yet come,"* which is in reference to the Revised Roman Empire that will come into existence when the Church is *"caught up"* or taken out of the earth. This kingdom, or empire, will *"continue a short space."* During the time of this *"short space,"* Antichrist will rise up and his kingdom, one of the ten kingdoms of the Revised Roman Empire, will wage war with three other kingdoms within the Revised Roman Empire. Earlier it was determined that the kingdom over which Antichrist is ruler is the Syrian Kingdom. He will *"subdue"* three kingdoms, i.e. Greece, Egypt and Turkey, thereby causing the old Grecian Empire to become revived. When Antichrist conquers these three kingdoms, he will become the ruler of the Revived Grecian Empire, **and it will be this kingdom that will be the *"eighth"* kingdom** and he, Antichrist, will go into *"perdition."* Therefore, *"the beast that was, and is not, even he is the eighth, and is of the seven…"* **is none other than the Grecian Empire, which will be revived!**

Verse 12 tells us that the *"ten horns…are ten kings, who have received no kingdom as yet, but receive power as kings one hour with the beast."* This is reiterating what was previously said, that none of the kings of the Revised Roman Empire would actually be ruler over any kingdom other than their own. However, Antichrist, ruler of the Syrian Kingdom, will war against three other kingdoms and *"subdue"* them. Therefore, the remaining six kingdoms will then rule as kings *"one hour with the beast.*" The fact that we are told they will rule "*one hour*" is indicative that they will merely rule only a very short time, during the last three and one half years, **with** Antichrist. Verse 13 tells us that they "*have one mind, and shall give their power and strength unto the beast.*" When the war drums are being heard, i.e. "*tidings out of the east and out of the north*" (Dan. 11:44), the remaining six kingdoms of the Revised Roman Empire then ally themselves with the "*beast*" by giving to him their "*power and strength.*" This is done because they want to be able to win this imminent war that is lurking on the horizon.

c. The Harlot Overthrown

"*These shall make war with the Lamb, and the Lamb shall overcome them; for he is Lord of lords, and King of kings, and they that are with him are called, and chosen, and faithful. And he saith unto me, The waters which thou sawest, where the harlot sitteth, are peoples, and multitudes, and nations, and tongues. And the ten horns which thou sawest upon the beast, these shall hate the harlot, and shall make her desolate and naked, and shall eat her flesh, and burn her with fire. For God hath put it in their hearts to fulfill his will, and to agree, and give their kingdom unto the beast, until the words of God shall be fulfilled. And the woman whom thou sawest is that great city, which reigneth over the kings of the earth.*" (Rev. 17:14-18)

In verse 14 we are shown a brief picture of the end of the Tribulation period when Jesus returns to the earth. We are told that He will overcome them that make war against Him. This verse merely is in anticipation of what is to come of those who are evil.

The angel now tells John in verse 15 that the "*waters which thou sawest...are peoples, and multitudes, and nations, and tongues.*" As stated earlier, the Apostate religion of the world will extend to every part of the world. This verse merely explains what the *"waters"* represented.

We are told that the *"ten horns....shall hate the harlot, and shall make her desolate and naked, and shall eat her flesh, and burn her with fire."* This is representative of the rulers of the Revised Roman Empire now rising up against the false religion and the false prophet. The false prophet will escape the punishment of the people and the rulers, but the Apostate religion will be destroyed. It is evident that possibly the churches of the false religion will be destroyed with fire. Also, it is possible that those in charge of each of the churches of the false religion may be killed and utterly destroyed to totally put an end to this hated religion. It would seem that now that Antichrist has become ruler over the entire Revised Roman Empire, he no longer needs the help of the Apostate Church to get him the power that he desires. Therefore, Apostate religion is totally destroyed and discarded. This is done because God has put it in the hearts of those who destroyed the false religion in order to fulfill His will. They are obviously unaware that they are doing what God wants them to do.

We are told that the *"woman whom thou sawest is that great city, which reigneth over the kings of the earth."* The reference is to Babylon in its religious form. The actual city is not destroyed yet, however, its Apostate religion is completely destroyed at this time. The *"great city"* is Babylon. Not that it is the actual city of Babylon, but it is the spiritual city of Babylon, which is believe to be Rome, which is the head of the Revised Roman Empire. Soon this city will fall, as shall be seen in the next chapter of Revelation. However, Babylon, the *"harlot,"* which is the Apostate Church, is now completely overthrown and no longer exists.

d. Babylon Destroyed

"And after these things I saw another angel come down from heaven, having great power, and the earth was made bright with his glory. And he cried mightily with a strong voice, saying, Babylon the great is fallen, is fallen, and is become the habitation of demons, and the hold of every foul spirit, and a cage of every unclean and hateful bird. For all nations have drunk of the wine of the wrath of her fornication, and the kings of the earth have committed fornication with her, and the merchants of the earth are grown rich through the abundance of her delicacies. And I heard another voice from heaven, saying, Come out of her, my people, that ye be not partakers of her sins, and that ye receive not her plagues; For her sins have reached unto heaven, and God hath remembered her iniquities. Reward her even as she rewarded you, and double unto her double according to her works; in the cup which she hath filled fill to her double. How much she hath glorified herself, and lived luxuriously, so much torment and sorrow give her; for she saith in her heart, I sit a queen, and am no widow, and shall see no sorrow. Therefore shall her plagues come in one day, death, and mourning, and famine, and she shall be utterly burned with fire; for strong is the Lord God who judgeth her." (Rev. 18:1-8)

The terminology *"after these things"* suggests that the events in Revelation 18 are different from those of Revelation 17, and they come at a later time. John says that he saw *"another angel come down from heaven,"* thus signifying that the angel here is a different angel than that in Revelation 17. The fact that we are told that when this angel comes, the *"earth was made bright with his glory"* is suggestive that he has authority to conduct some great work on God's behalf.

Earlier in Revelation 14:8, we were given the prophecy of the fall of Babylon. Here in 18:2 the angel repeats almost word for word, *"Babylon the great is fallen, is fallen...."* It would seem that the repetitious use of the verb, *"is fallen,"* signifies the finality of Babylon's doom. In chapter 17 we dealt with the harlot, who represented Babylon in its religious form. The harlot is destroyed by Antichrist after he enters into the temple and sets himself up as God and demands that all people worship him and receive his mark. He no longer needs the help of the Apostate Church to get him to where he desires to be politically or spiritually. Therefore, it is at the hand of mankind, the people and leaders of the earth that are tired of the whole of the Apostate religion, that destroys religious Babylon.

Antichrist and his followers destroy religious Babylon and begin a new worldwide worship of the ruler of the Revised Roman Empire and the Revived Grecian Empire. It would seem that the false religion of Apostasy might have begun its climb to greatness at the beginning of the first half of the Tribulation period. Then in the middle of the period, or the beginning of the last half of the Tribulation, the events of chapter 17 were dealt with. The events of Revelation 18 take place during the last half of the Tribulation period. Therefore, the events in Revelation 18 deal with Babylon in its political form, as well as its economic character.

We are told that Babylon will become the *"habitation of demons, and the hold of every foul spirit, and a cage of every unclean and hateful bird."* The word *"hold"* in this verse means **prison**. Therefore, it would seem that Babylon would be full of demons and foul, or evil sprits, characterized by the unclean and hateful birds. This is a type of judgment upon Babylon and the people therein.

Babylon in its political form will have had many evil and sinister relationships with other nations throughout the world. Thus we are told, *"For all nations have drunk the wine of the wrath of her fornication, and the kings of the earth have committed fornication with her, and the merchants of the earth are grown rich through the abundance of her delicacies."* In chapter 17 we were told that the harlot was *"arrayed in purple and scarlet* color, and bedecked with gold and precious stones and pearls, having a golden cup in her hand..." This was significant of the wealth that was gained by the Apostate Church through its wickedness. After the destruction of the Apostate Church, the wealth would be taken over by Antichrist's political system. The dealings that Antichrist will have with other nations throughout the world will also bring in much wealth. Therefore, Babylon will be full of wealth and those that deal with Babylon, i.e. the "merchants of the earth," will become wealthy.

In verse 4 John hears "another voice from heaven, saying, Come out of her, my people, that ye be not partakers of her sins, and that ye receive not of her plagues." God's people are instructed to leave Babylon in much the same way the Israelites were instructed to leave Babylon in earlier times before judgment was passed upon the city. (Jer. 51:45) The people of God are commanded to leave Babylon before judgment comes, otherwise they may become partakers of the sins and the plagues that are to come upon her. The plagues are in reference to the bowl judgments, and especially the seventh bowl judgment that comes upon Babylon. (See Rev. 16:17-21)

Verses 5-8 speak about the judgments to come upon Babylon. We are told that "her sins have reached unto heaven, and God hath remembered her iniquities." This refers to the fact that the sins of Antichrist's political system have become as terrible as possible and now God has come into remembrance of "her iniquities." We are told that the judgments are to be twice as much as what she has done to God's people. The angel says, "Reward her even as she rewarded you, and double unto her double according to her works; in the cup which she filled fill to her double." There is to be no mercy on Antichrist's political system or the people involved in it. Those that worship the beast and have taken his mark will not find comfort or peace. The judgment of the seventh bowl will be poured out upon all and they will suffer tremendously.

Antichrist will think, however, that because he has gained so much wealth and is living so luxuriously that he will not be effected by the plagues. But we are told that the fifth bowl judgment will be poured out *"upon the throne of the beast,"* thus he and all within his kingdom who worship him and have received his mark will suffer the plagues that come upon them. The fact that we are told that *"her plagues come in one day, death, and mourning, and famine, and she shall be utterly burned with fire,"* is indicative that suddenly the plagues will come and they will not escape God's wrath.

1. Earth Dwellers Mourn Babylon's Destruction

"And the kings of the earth, who have committed fornication and lived luxuriously with her, shall bewail her, and lament for her, when they shall see the smoke of her burning, Standing afar off for the fear of her torment, saying, Alas, alas, that great city, Babylon, that mighty city! For in one hour is thy judgment come. And the merchants of the earth shall weep and mourn over her; for no man buyeth their merchandise any more: The merchandise of gold, and silver, and precious stones, and pearls, and fine linen, and purple, and silk, and scarlet, and all thyine wood, and all kinds of vessels of ivory, and all kinds of vessels of most precious wood, and of bronze, and iron, and marble, And cinnamon, and incense, and ointments, and frankincense, and wine, and oil, and fine flour, and wheat, and cattle, and sheep, and horses, and chariots, and slaves, and souls of men. And the fruits that thy soul lusted after are departed from thee, and all things which were dainty and sumptuous are departed from thee, and thou shalt find them no more at all. The merchants of these things, who made rich by her, shall stand afar off for the fear of her torment, weeping and wailing, And saying, Alas, alas, that great city, that was clothed in fine linen, and purple, and scarlet, and bedecked with gold, and precious stones, and pearls! For in one hour so great riches are come to nothing. And every shipmaster, and all the company of ships, and sailors and as many as trade by sea, stood

afar off, And cried when they saw the smoke of her burning, saying, What city is like unto this great city? And they cast dust on their heads, and cried, weeping and wailing, saying, Alas, alas, that great city, in which were made rich all that had ships in the sea by reason of her costliness! For in one hour is she made desolate." (Rev. 18:9-19)

In the verses above we can see that all the kings and merchants who have gotten rich because of the sins of Babylon are really having a pity party because they can no longer buy, sell or trade and gain more wealth. The destruction of Babylon will be at the time of Jesus' Second Coming to the earth. Many times throughout the above verses we see the statement that Babylon has fallen in *"one hour."* The political system of Babylon will no longer exist. Those that dwell within the city will die because of the plagues and the brightness of Jesus' coming. Many will stand afar off and mourn the loss of so much beauty and riches. We are told that the people stand afar off *"for the fear of her torment."* They stand watching the destruction and cry and wail because the great city of Babylon is destroyed and burning. They fear the torment because they don't want to get caught in the destruction.

Throughout verses 9 through 19 we are told no less than three times that Babylon is judged, come to nothing and made desolate in *"one hour."* We see that even though Babylon has said in her heart, *"I sit a queen, and am no widow, and shall see no sorrow,"* (Rev. 18:7) she is suddenly made a ruined city in *"one hour."* Those that mourn her loss cry out, *"What city is like unto this great city?"* They have lost the prize they so much enjoyed, all in *"one hour."* God's great judgment has come and the iniquities of political Babylon has been judged with righteous judgment.

2. Heaven Rejoices Over Babylon's Fall

"Rejoice over her, thou heaven, and ye holy apostles and prophets; for God hath avenged you on her. And a mighty angel took up a stone like a great millstone, and cast it into the sea, saying, Thus with violence shall that great city, Babylon, be thrown down, and shall be found no more at all. And the voice of harpers, and minstrels, and flute players, and trumpeters shall be heard no more at all in thee; and no craftsman, of whatever craft he be, shall be found any more in thee; and the sound of the millstone shall be heard no more at all in thee; And the light of a lamp shall shine no more at all in thee; and the voice of the bridegroom and the bride shall be heard no more at all in thee; for thy merchants were the great men of the earth; for by thy sorceries were all nations deceived. And in her was found the blood of the prophets, and of saints, and of all that were slain upon the earth." (Rev. 18:20-24)

In the verses above we are told *"Rejoice over her, thou heaven, and ye holy apostles and prophets; for God hath avenged you on her."* While we are told that the people on earth are crying and mourning over the fall of Babylon, all of heaven rejoices over her fall. We are told that an angel *"took up a stone like a great millstone, and cast it into the sea, saying, Thus with violence shall that great city, Babylon, be thrown down, and shall be found no more at all."* This is significant of the sudden destruction of Babylon. Never again will the earth have a city or political power such as this. Never again will people make a joyful noise in its streets. Never again will merchants, craftsmen or tradesmen do their evil business such as before. Never again will there be heard the joy of marriage in the city. We can see that all the *"great men of the earth"* will no longer conduct any business there again. All wickedness and iniquity will be utterly destroyed by the brightness of Jesus' coming to the earth. At this time, which is at the end of the Tribulation period, all sin will be destroyed. The only people left on the earth will be

153

those who have not taken the mark of the beast or who have not worshipped his image. There will be many that have not even heard of Antichrist that will yet remain on the earth and have the chance to enter into the Millennial kingdom. They will be given the chance to choose whom they will serve before the beginning of the Millennial period. (This will be discussed in a later chapter.) But Babylon will never again be found on the earth.

We are told that *"in her was found the blood of prophets, and of saints, and of all that were slain upon the earth."* The fact that we are told that in Babylon was found the blood of the prophets, saints and all that were slain upon the earth is indicative of the evil within this political power. They are charged with the death of all that have lost their lives because of their testimony in Christ. Therefore, the wicked men of this evil Babylon are suddenly judged with God's righteous judgment and are destroyed by His power.

3. Heaven Rejoices Over The Destruction Of The Harlot

"And after these things I heard a great voice of many people in heaven, saying, Hallelujah! Salvation, and glory, and honor, and power, unto the Lord, our God; For true and righteous are his judgments; for he hath judged the great harlot, who did corrupt the earth with her fornication, and hath avenged the blood of his servants at her hand. And again they said, Hallelujah! And her smoke rose up forever and ever. And the four and twenty elders and the four living creatures fell down and worshiped God that sat on the throne, saying Amen. Hallelujah! And a voice came out of the throne, saying, Praise our God, all ye his servants, and ye that fear him, both small and great. And I heard, as it were, the voice of a great multitude, and like the voice of many waters, and like the voice of mighty peals of thunder, saying, Hallelujah! For the Lord God omnipotent reigneth." (Rev. 19:1-6)

John now states that *"after these things I heard a great voice of many people in heaven…"* which seems to be in reference to the same group as in Rev. 7:9 who are the Gentile multitude that gave their lives during the Great Tribulation period for their testimony of Christ. They rejoice over the fact that Babylon in all its forms has been destroyed. We are told that *"her smoke rose up forever and ever,"* a reference of Babylon, the Harlot, forever destroyed.

God's judgments are said to be *"true and righteous."* The *"harlot"* which, as was found earlier, was the Apostate religion of the world, and is totally destroyed. False religion deceives many throughout the world and because of her *"fornication"* God sends His righteous and true judgments upon the *"harlot."* It is because of the *"harlot"* that many saints are killed, therefore, God's judgment is justified.

We are told that the *"four and twenty elders and the four living creatures fell down and worshiped God that sat on the throne, saying, Amen. Hallelujah!"* These were first introduced to us in Rev. 4 and they forever worship God. They are seen as adding their praise to God for His true and righteous judgments.

A voice is heard that *"came out of the throne, saying, Praise our God, all ye his servants, and ye that fear him, both small and great."* Some believe this *"voice"* to be the voice of God Himself. Rather, it is more likely the voice of some angel near the throne, for he says, *"Praise our God."* He is referring to God; therefore, it must not be God that speaks. The invitation to praise God is to all peoples both *"small and great."* In verse six it seems that all the people join together in the praise and to John, it sounds as if it were *"the voice of a great multitude, and like the voice of many waters, and like the voice of mighty peals of thunder."* They all join in unison *"Hallelujah! For the Lord God omnipotent reigneth."* God is worthy of our praise!

5. The Battle Of Armageddon

The Vision of Armageddon was discussed earlier. (See subparagraph 2, g, 5) For many years we have heard of this great battle. We have seen movies and read books pertaining to the greatest war that will ever be fought on this earth. Of all the wars that have previously been fought and won or lost, none will come near the magnitude of the war in Armageddon. Throughout this book, I have discussed many events leading up to this great war. When this battle is fought, it will be the most spectacular of all wars, for it will be not only a physical battle between men, but it will be a spiritual battle between evil and righteousness. As Christians, we know the outcome of this battle. Jesus will be the victor! Satan and all his followers will be totally defeated.

The battle of Armageddon coincides with the Second Coming of Christ. All of the events contained in the judgments of Revelation lead up to this great event. The war that Antichrist fights during the last half of the Tribulation period will bring all armies of the world to this place to do battle. Jesus will come and the war will focus on trying to prevent Him from establishing His kingdom on earth. Antichrist and the false prophet will meet their end here, as will the followers of Antichrist. Jesus will be the victor and He will usher in the greatest time of peace on earth!

a. The Three Unclean Spirits

"And I saw three loathsome spirits like frogs, leaping from the mouth of the dragon and from the mouth of the beast and from the mouth of the false prophet. For really they are the spirits of demons that perform signs (wonders, miracles). And they go forth to the rulers and leaders all over the world, to gather them together for war on the great day of God the Almighty. Lo, I am coming like a thief!

Blessed — happy, to be envied — is he who stays awake (alert) and who guards his clothes so that he may not be naked and (have the shame of being) seen exposed! And they gathered them together at the place which in Hebrew is called Armageddon." (Rev. 16:13-16 Amp. Bible)

John tells us that he *"saw three loathsome spirits like frogs, leaping from the mouth of the dragon and from the mouth of the beast and from the mouth of the false prophet."* These *"loathsome"* spirits are called *"unclean"* spirits in the King James Version. The fact that they are said to come from the mouths of the dragon, beast and false prophet suggests that these are the unholy trinity, which is opposite of the Holy Trinity of God, Jesus and the Holy Spirit. The *"dragon"* represents Satan, the unholy opposite of God, the *"beast"* represents Antichrist, the unholy opposite of Jesus, and the *"false prophet"* is the unholy opposite of the Holy Spirit. Therefore, it is obvious that these three individuals are the rulers of evil and are in alliance with each other.

We are told the three unclean spirits are really *"the spirits of demons."* They are said to be able to perform miracles or wonders in the sight of men. These demons are dispatched to *"the rulers and leaders all over the world, to gather them together for war..."* and they are evidently very convincing, for they are successful in doing this as we see in verse 16. By some means of miracles these demon spirits are able to convince the leaders and rulers throughout the world to send their armies to Armageddon to fight a war. Possibly they deceive the leaders and rulers with lies, and by their miracles they provide proof for their lies in order to convince them to join in the war. It is also possible that these unclean spirits are able to cause the leaders and rulers of the world to begin to think of overthrowing the *"beast"* or Antichrist, since it is evident that his empire is decaying. Therefore, they would attempt to wage war against him, and against each other, to gain higher honors or political status. Thus it seems that the armies of the entire world will be represented during the war of Armageddon.

In verse 15 the Lord says *"Lo, I am going to come like a thief!"* This is indicative of the fact that during this ongoing war, the leaders and rulers of the world are going to be totally surprised by His coming. They will not know that Jesus is coming until He suddenly appears. When Jesus comes, the war will be shifted from that of against each other to fighting against Christ. They will be totally destroyed by the brightness of His coming. We are told *"Blessed—happy, to be envied—is he who stays awake (alert) and who guards his clothes so that he may not be naked and have the shame of being seen exposed!"* These who are *"awake"* are those who have denied Antichrist and have followed after Jesus. Only these will survive this war. Only the followers of Christ and those who have not taken the mark of the beast or have not worshipped his image will remain.

We are told that the armies of the world are gathered *"together at the place which in Hebrew is called Armageddon."* This is a place in the area of Megiddo. It was mentioned earlier that the armies of the world will come together in a place that is said to be *"1600 stadia."* (Rev.14:20 NIV) It was said that this distance is approximately 200 miles. Therefore, it seems that the armies of the world will be gathered together and they will station themselves within this 200-mile area throughout the valley of Megiddo. The armies will be in and all around Jerusalem for a distance of 200 miles in either direction.

b. Climax: The Battle Of Armageddon Coincides With The Second Coming Of Christ

"Then I saw a single angel stationed in the sun's light, and with a mighty voice he shouted to all the birds that fly across the sky,

Come, gather yourselves together for the great supper of God, That you may feast on the flesh of rulers, the flesh of generals and captains, the flesh of powerful and mighty men, the flesh of horses and their riders, and the flesh of all humanity, both free and slave, both small and great! Then I saw the beast and the rulers and leaders of the earth with their troops mustered to go into battle and make war against Him Who is mounted on the horse and against His troops." (Rev. 19:17-19 Amp. Bible)

John now sees a *"single angel stationed in the sun's light."* The King James Version says that the angel is *"standing in the sun."* This angel perhaps outshines the light of the sun and is visible to John in this vision. The angel invites the *"birds"* to gather themselves *"together for the great supper of God."* This supper mentioned here is not the marriage supper of the Lamb as some suggest. Rather it is the gathering of the birds of prey to eat of the flesh of those fallen in battle. There is no respecter of persons here, for we are told that the flesh of all the rulers, generals and captains, the flesh of the powerful and mighty men, the flesh of the horses and their riders, and the flesh of all humanity, both free and slave, both small and great are to be eaten. The birds of prey will feast throughout all of the area of this battle, for there will be the bodies of slain men and women for them to devour.

We are told the *"beast and the rulers and leaders of the earth with their troops mustered to go into battle and make war against Him Who is mounted on the horse and against His troops."* At the time that all armies of the world are gathered together for this war, they will evidently be engaged in battle against Israel for a time. (Zech. 14:2) Suddenly, Jesus comes riding a white horse (Rev. 19:11) and His troops (Rev. 19:14) are with Him. The battle then changes from that of warring against each other to engaging Jesus and the saints when He comes. As stated earlier, Jesus will be the victor in this war. The King of Kings and Lord of Lords will destroy all those who are the followers of Antichrist. Also stated earlier, this war coincides with the Second Coming of Christ.

Chapter Seven
THE SECOND COMING OF CHRIST

Following the events of the Tribulation period, which literally comes to a climax, the event we call the Second Coming of Christ is ushered in. The Second Coming of Christ has been confused many times with that of His coming to Rapture the Church. While some believe that the Second Coming is the time when Jesus will Rapture the saints of the Church Age, this is not true. At the time of the Rapture, we are told that He will come *"in the air"* (1 Thess. 4:17), whereas at His Second Coming, He will place His feet upon the Mount of Olives (Zech. 14:4). At the time of the Rapture, Jesus comes to carry away His bride, the Church (St. Matt. 25:1-13; Eph. 5:27,32), whereas at His Second Coming, He comes to destroy the wicked (Rev. 19:21). Therefore, the Second Coming of Christ is a separate event from that of His coming to Rapture the Church.

A. Prophecies Of The Second Coming Of Christ

"For I know that my redeemer liveth, and that he shall stand at the latter day upon the earth." (Job 19:25)

"And his feet shall stand in that day upon the Mount of Olives, which is before Jerusalem on the east, and the Mount of Olives shall cleave in its midst toward the east and toward the west, and there

shall be a very great valley; and half of the mountain shall remove toward the north, and half of it toward the south." (Zech. 14:4)

"And then shall appear the sign of the Son of man in heaven; and then shall all the tribes of the earth mourn, and they shall see the Son of man coming in the clouds of heaven with power and great glory." (St. Matt. 24:30)

"And to you who are troubled, rest with us, when the Lord Jesus shall be revealed from heaven with his mighty angels, In flaming fire taking vengeance on them that know not God, and that obey not the gospel of our Lord Jesus Christ." (2 Thess. 1:8-9)

"Let no one deceive or beguile you in any way, for that day will not come except the apostasy comes first—that is, unless the (predicted) great falling away of those who have professed to be Christians has come—and the man of lawlessness (sin) is revealed, who is the son of doom (of perdition),....And then the lawless one (the Antichrist) will be revealed and the Lord Jesus will slay him with the breath of His mouth and bring him to an end by His appearing at His coming." (2 Thess. 2:3, 8 Amp. Bible)

"Behold, he cometh with clouds, and every eye shall see him, and they also who pierced him; and all kindreds of the earth shall wail because of him. Even so. Amen." (Rev. 1:7)

B. The Purpose Of The Second Coming Of Christ

The purpose of the Second Coming of Christ is two-fold. First, Jesus comes to establish His earthly kingdom. In so doing, He must deal with the rebellion of the wicked on the earth. Secondly, the purpose of His coming is to destroy Antichrist and the False Prophet and to place Satan in prison for the duration of the Millennial period, or 1000 years. Jesus' coming is at the time when all the armies of Antichrist and the world are gathered together in the valley of Megiddo to do battle against Israel.

However, the armies of the earth are also there for the purpose of warring against Israel and possibly against Antichrist perhaps to displace him from his fast declining power. When Jesus appears, all of the armies of the earth then turn their attention to doing battle against the *"KING OF KINGS, AND LORD OF LORDS."* (Rev. 19:16)

1. Christ's Coming In Glory

"And I saw heaven opened and, behold, a white horse; and he that sat upon him was called Faithful and True, and inrighteousness he doth judge and make war. His eyes were like a flame of fire, and on his head were many crowns; and he had a name written, that no man knew, but he himself. And he was clothed with a vesture dipped in blood; and his name is called The Word of God." (Rev. 19:11-13)

Jesus will come to the earth in *"righteous"* judgment. As previously stated, at the time of His coming to Rapture the saints of the Church Age, He comes *"in the air."* (1 Thess. 4:17) However, at His Second Coming, He will come to the earth. (Zech. 14:4) At this time of His coming to the earth, He will come to bring judgment upon those who are wicked. He does not come to bless. Rather He comes to *"make war."* This coming coincides with the battle of Armageddon, and with the final bowl judgement. At this time, He will destroy political Babylon, those who are *"beast"* worshippers and who have received the *"mark"* of the beast, and all those *"whose names were not written in the book of life from the foundation of the world."* (Rev. 17:8) At this time the *"beast"*, or Antichrist, and his *"false prophet,"* together will be *"cast alive into a lake of fire burning with brimstone."* (Rev. 19:20) Furthermore, it will be at this coming when Satan will be bound and cast into the *"bottomless pit"* for a period of a *"thousand years."* (Rev 20:2-3) Jesus comes at this time to the earth to war against evil and He will become the Victor!

In the Book of Zechariah, chapter 14, we are told that *"all nations"* will be gathered together to do battle *"against Jerusalem."* (vs.2) *"Then shall the Lord go forth, and fight against those nations, as when he fought in the day of battle. And his feet shall stand in that day upon the Mount of Olives, which is before Jerusalem on the east, and the Mount of Olives shall cleave in its midst toward the east and toward the west, and there shall be a very great valley; and half of the mountain shall remove toward the north, and half of it toward the south."* (vss. 3-4) The Mount of Olives is the place where Jesus left this earth on the day of His ascension into heaven. (Acts 1:9-12) It will be at this Mount of Olives where we are told that He will return and *"his feet shall stand in that day."* When He comes, we are told that the mountain will *"cleave in its midst toward the east and toward the west."* This is representative of His glorious power and authority.

We are further told of Jesus' Second Coming in St. Matthew 24:27-31. Many have misunderstood and thought that these verses refer to the Rapture of the Church. However, this cannot be so because it says, *"Immediately after the tribulation of those days,"* which is in reference to the period of time after the trials that will come upon the earth, **after** the Church has been *"caught up."* Remember, Jesus said *"Because thou hast kept the word of my patience, I will also keep thee from the hour of temptation, which shall come upon all the world, to try them that dwell upon the earth."* (Rev. 3:10) He has promised the saints of the Church Age, that because they have kept His Word and because they have forsaken all to follow Him, He will keep them from the *"hour of temptation"*, meaning the period of the Tribulation.

The *"elect"* spoken of in St. Matthew 24:31 are the saints of the Tribulation period who have suffered death because of their testimony of Christ. Also, the *"elect"* in this verse represents all the saints in heaven, both of the old Testament and of the Church Age, along with these saints of the Tribulation period, who will join Jesus at His Second Coming and war against the wicked on earth.

The fact that we are told that *"His eyes were like a flame of fire, and on his head were many crowns; and he had a name written, that no man knew, but he himself,"* suggests that Jesus comes in righteous judgment of the wicked on the earth. The *"many crowns"* on His head suggests His priestly sovereignty, and the name *"that no man knew, but he himself"* is a name that is not yet revealed. We are told that He is *"clothed with a vesture dipped in blood,"* which is probably in reference to His divine judgment upon mankind. Jesus' name is called *"The Word of God"* for He was, as spoken in St. John 1:1-2, *"...the Word, and the Word was with God, and the Word was God. The same was in the beginning with God."*

2. The *"KING OF KINGS, AND LORD OF LORDS"*

"And the armies that were in heaven followed him upon white horses, clothed in fine linen, white and clean. And out of his mouth goeth a sharp sword, that with it he should smite the nations, and he shall rule them with a rod of iron; and he treadeth the winepress of the fierceness and wrath of Almighty God. And he hath on his vesture and on his thigh a name written, KING OF KINGS, AND LORD OF LORDS." (Rev. 19:14-16)

Here we are told that *"the armies of heaven followed him upon white horses, clothed in fine linen, white and clean."* Some people try to limit this to only the saints of the Church Age because of the fact that we are told that these will receive robes of righteousness, clean and white. However, it is far more preferable to include the saints of the Old Testament, who were resurrected at the time of Jesus' resurrection and who accompanied Him to paradise when He ascended to Heaven.

Furthermore, it is probable that the saints who have died because of their testimony of Christ during the Tribulation period may be included in this great army. It is also a certainty that the holy angels will accompany Jesus at His Second Coming.

We are further told that *"out of his mouth goeth a sharp sword, that with it he should smite the nations, and he shall rule them with a rod of iron..."* As stated earlier, all nations of the earth will be gathered together in Megiddo to do battle. (Zech. 14 :2-3; Rev. 16:13-16) At this time, when Jesus comes to the earth, He will come to destroy and to wipe away all sin and wickedness. Therefore, the *"sharp sword"* spoken of here is symbolic of an instrument of war with which Jesus uses to *"smite the nations, and he shall rule them with a rod of iron."* Once the wicked armies of the earth are destroyed at Armageddon, and Satan is chained in the *"bottomless pit"* for a one thousand year period, and all wickedness has been destroyed, those remaining on the earth will be required to accept Jesus as Lord or they will not be allowed to enter into His Millennial Kingdom. I sometimes like to use "play on words" here and state that Jesus will become the ultimate world dictator. In reality, Jesus will rule the entire earth with a *"rod of iron."* This *"rod of iron"* is symbolic of His absolute, unyielding righteous rule that will be imposed upon all who are in the earth after His Second Coming. This will be a welcomed and greatly desired righteous government for those living on the earth during this time.

When Jesus comes at this time, He *"treadeth the winepress of the fierceness and wrath of Almighty God."* This is suggestive of the terrible and divine judgment of God upon those who have cursed Him and those who have decided to turn away from Him. All wickedness will be destroyed. The *"beast,"* or Antichrist, and the *"false prophet"* will be *"cast alive into a lake of fire burning with brimstone."* (Rev.19:20) Satan will be caught and bound in chains and cast into the *"bottomless pit"* to be imprisoned there for one thousand years. (Rev. 20:1-3) All those who have followed after the *"beast"* and the *"false prophet"* and worshipped the *"image of the beast"* will be killed at Armageddon. Those remaining on the earth will be those who have not adhered to the demands of Antichrist. They will become judged at the time of the judgment of the nations (more on this in the next chapter). They will become "citizens" of the new government that will be established when Jesus comes, and they will conform to His righteous rule.

Jesus will rule the entire earth and take His rightful place as King. We are told that He *"hath on his vesture and on his thigh a name written, KING OF KINGS, AND LORD OF LORDS."* Jesus will rule the earth in righteousness! People throughout the earth will come to worship Him every year. After He comes to the earth and destroys all wickedness, He will establish His earthly kingdom, which will be without sin. This will be a time of glorious praise unto our *"KING OF KINGS, AND LORD OF LORDS!!"*

3. Coincides With The Battle Of Armageddon

"And I saw an angel standing in the sun; and he cried with a loud voice, saying to all the fowls that fly in the midst of heaven, Come and gather yourselves together unto the supper of the great God, That ye may eat the flesh of kings, and the flesh of captains, and the flesh of mighty men, and the flesh of horses and of them that sit on them, and the flesh of all men, both free and enslaved, both small and great. And I saw the beast, and the kings of the earth, and their armies, gathered together to make war against him that sat on the horse, and against his army." (Rev. 19:17-19)

This was discussed in the previous chapter, however, I believe that it bares repeating. I think it is important to note that at the time of Jesus' Second Coming, all that are beast worshippers will be destroyed.

John now sees a *"single angel stationed in the sun's light."* The King James Version says that the angel is *"standing in the sun."* This angel perhaps outshines the light of the sun and is visible to John in this vision. The angel invites the *"birds"* to gather themselves *"together for the great supper of God."* This supper mentioned here is not the marriage supper of the Lamb as some suggest. Rather it is the gathering of the birds of prey to eat of the flesh of those fallen in battle. There is no respecter of persons here, for we are told that the flesh of all the rulers, generals and captains, the flesh of the powerful and mighty men, the flesh of the horses and their riders, and the flesh of all humanity, both free and slave, both small and great are to be eaten. The birds of prey will feast throughout all of the area of this battle, for there will be the bodies of slain men and women for them to devour.

We are told the *"beast and the rulers and leaders of the earth with their troops mustered to go into battle and make war against Him Who is mounted on the horse and against His troops."* At the time that all armies of the world are gathered together for this war, they will evidently be engaged in battle against Israel for a time. (Zech. 14:2) Suddenly, Jesus comes riding a white horse (Rev. 19:11) and His troops (Rev. 19:14) are with Him. The battle then changes from that of warring against each other to engaging Jesus and the saints when He comes. As stated earlier, Jesus will be the victor in this war. The *"KING OF KING, AND LORD OF LORDS"* will destroy all those who are the followers of Antichrist. Also stated earlier, this war coincides with the Second Coming of Christ.

4. Doom Of The Beast And The False Prophet

"And the beast was taken, and with him the false prophet that wrought miracles before him, with which he deceived them that had received the mark of the beast, and them that worshiped his image. These both were cast alive into a lake of fire burning with brimstone." (Rev. 19:20)

The *"lake of fire burning with brimstone"* is the final eternal dwelling of all that do not follow Christ. Here we are told that the *"beast"* of Rev. 13:1-10 and the *"false prophet,"* the second beast of Rev. 13:11-16, are both *"cast alive"* into this *"lake of fire burning with brimstone."* This *"beast"* of Rev. 13:1-10 is none other than Antichrist. He and his false prophet are taken *"alive"* and cast into eternal torment, where they will be throughout all eternity. These two will precede even Satan, who will be cast into the *"bottomless pit"* for one thousand years. (Rev. 20:1-3) After the *"one thousand years"* are finished, he will be cast into the lake of fire *"where the beast and the false prophet are."* (Rev. 20:10) It will be this same *"lake of fire"* that all sinners from the beginning of time will ultimately be cast.

Some people believe that when a sinner dies, he is sent to purgatory where he is given a chance to redeem himself and earn his right to go to heaven. **There is no such place for sinners!** When sinners die, they go to Hades, which is the dwelling of demons, where they await the time of their resurrection unto judgment. When they are resurrected unto judgment, they will stand before God and be judged for their sinful lives on earth and be cast into the *"lake of fire"* for their wrong doings. (Rev. 20:11-15)

5. Doom Of Kings And Armies

"And the remnant were slain with the sword of him that sat upon the horse, which sword proceeded out of his mouth; and all the fowls were filled with their flesh." (Rev. 19:21)

In this verse we are told that the *"remnant were slain with the sword of him that sat upon the horse, which sword proceeded out of his mouth."* Jesus now kills those that were not killed by the armies and by the capturing of Antichrist and his false prophet. Not one person will escape this judgment. No matter

169

what status people have in life on earth, all evil will be totally destroyed at Jesus' Second Coming. This judgment is so final that we are told that the *"fowls were filled with their flesh."* All those that rose against Christ in battle will be totally destroyed by the *"sword of him that sat upon the horse, which sword proceeded out of his mouth."* Those that survive at His coming will be those who have not worshipped the *"beast"* or received his mark. Those who have decided to serve Jesus in a time of terrible affliction and who have survived will continue to live on the earth for *"one thousand years."* (Zech. 14:9-21)

6. Satan Bound For One Thousand Years

"And I saw an angel come down from heaven, having the key of the bottomless pit and a great chain in his hand. And he laid hold on the dragon, that old serpent, who is the Devil and Satan, and bound him a thousand years, And cast him into the bottomless pit, and shut him up, and set a seal upon him, that he should deceive the nations no more, till the thousand years should be fulfilled; and after that he must be loosed a little season." (Rev. 20:1-3)

These verses have caused many disputes of scholars of prophecy for many years. Some believe that these verses should be interpreted in a symbolical view, while others believe they should be interpreted in the literal view. The Word of God is, in my opinion, to be understood to be the literal truth. The Word says what it means and means what it says. Therefore, it would seem to be preferable that we interpret these verses in the literal view.

John sees in this vision, an *"angel come down from heaven, having the key of the bottomless pit and a great chain in his hand. And he laid hold on the dragon, that old serpent, who is the Devil and Satan, and bound him a thousand years."* The fact that this angel is said to have the key of the bottomless pit denotes that he is sent to perform the task of binding Satan. He has a *"great chain"* in his hand with which he is to bind Satan. It is evident that Satan will be powerless to prevent this angel from binding him. Satan will be bound with this chain and imprisoned in the bottomless pit for a period of *"one thousand years."* The angel places a *"seal upon him, that he should deceive the nations no more, till the thousand years should be fulfilled; and after that he must be loosed a little season."* During this *"one thousand years"* Satan will not be able to deceive the nations or any person. He will be totally bound in this prison for the full one thousand years. This event will be discussed in more detail in a later chapter.

7. The Completion Of The First Resurrection

"And I saw thrones, and they sat upon them, and judgment was given unto them; and I saw the souls of them that were beheaded for the witness of Jesus, and for the word of God, and who had not worshiped the beast, neither his image, neither had received his mark upon their foreheads, or in their hands; and they lived and reigned with Christ a thousand years. But the rest of the dead lived not again until the thousand years were finished. This is the first resurrection. Blessed and holy is he that hath part in the first resurrection; on such the second death hath no power, but they shall be priests of God and of Christ, and shall reign with him a thousand years." (Rev. 20:4-6)

When Satan becomes bound in the *"bottomless pit"* and is no longer free to deceive for *"one thousand years,"* then there will be people who will continue to live with Jesus on the earth. John says that he *"saw thrones, and they sat upon them, and judgment was given unto them."* Who are these that are sitting upon thrones and have been given judgment? It is the opinion of this writer that they are the saints of the Church Age, as well as the saints of the Old Testament and the saints who were martyred or killed for their testimony of Christ during the Tribulation period. These will *"reign"* with Christ for *"one thousand years!"* However, it will be the saints of the Tribulation period who have survived and are still alive when Jesus establishes His earthly kingdom that will *"live"* with Him for *"one thousand years."* The fact that we are told that *"the souls of them that were beheaded for the witness of Jesus, and for the word of God, and who had not worshiped the beast, neither his image, neither had received his mark upon their foreheads, or in their hands; and they lived and reigned with Christ a thousand years"* is evident that the Tribulation saints will live again in the same manner as do the saints of the Church Age and the Old Testament saints after resurrection. All the saints of the Old Testament period, and all the saints of the Church Age, and all the saints who will have died during the Tribulation period will live and reign *"with Christ a thousand years."* But it will be those saints who have survived the trials of the Tribulation period and who are still alive when Jesus comes to the earth that will continue to live in the flesh and bone (earthly) body with Christ for the thousand years.

We are told that *"the rest of the dead lived not again until the thousand years were finished."* This is in reference to the sinners who are now dead and who never turned their lives over to Jesus. All sinners from the beginning of time are referred to here. They do not have part in the *"first resurrection."* The sinners are not the *"blessed and holy."* They will take part in the *"second death."* It is only the saints of God of the Old Testament, the Church Age and the Tribulation period that have part in the first resurrection. These are resurrected to be able to spend eternity with Christ. Many of those who are still alive on the earth during the *"thousand years"* will also have part in this first resurrection, in that, many of them will not be deceived by Satan when he is *"loosed for a little season."* (Rev. 20:3) They will then be changed in the same manner as will be the saints who are alive at the time of the Rapture of the Church. (This will be discussed more in a later chapter.)

C. The Result Of The Second Coming Of Christ

The result of the Second Coming of Christ is the establishing of His kingdom on earth. When He comes to the earth, He comes at the time when all the armies of the earth have been gathered together to do battle against Jerusalem. (Zech. 14:2) His coming coincides with the seventh seal judgment, which contains the seven trumpet judgments and the seven bowl judgments, which climaxes at the seventh bowl judgment. His coming coincides with the marriage supper of the Lamb and ushers in the millennial period.

When Jesus comes to the earth at His Second Coming, He will destroy all wickedness. Satan will be defeated and bound for a period of one thousand years. All the saints of the Old Testament, the Church Age and the saints who were killed during the Tribulation period will live again and reign with Jesus. Those who are still alive and who have not worshiped the *"beast"* or his image and who have not received his mark will live with Christ on earth for one thousand years. The result of the Second Coming of Christ will be the triumphant beginning of Jesus' reign on earth as *"KING OF KINGS, AND LORD OF LORDS!"*

Chapter Eight
THE MILLENNIAL KINGDOM

The Millennial Reign. Fact or fiction? Will there be a time when there will be total peace on earth? We have dreamed of universal peace. Some world leaders have worked toward world peace. Preachers have preached about this time of peace. Teachers have taught about it. But will it ever become reality? According to the Word of God, the answer is a resounding yes!

Did you know that every child of God from Adam unto the end of the Tribulation period will either live with Christ or they will reign with Him during the Millennial period? This is true! Those who have lived their lives and then died will reign with Jesus as kings and priests. Those Christians who are *"caught up"* to be with Jesus at the time of the Rapture will be among these who will reign with Him. However, those people who will still be living on the earth at the time the Tribulation period comes to a close, these will continue to live with Jesus for the one thousand years of the Millennial period. There will be people who will actually become older than Methuselah living on this earth some day! In this chapter, this event, the Millennial period, will be discussed. Those who will be living on the earth during this great period of time will also be discussed.

A. Prophecies Of The Millennial Kingdom

There are scriptures in the Bible that predicts the future Millennial Kingdom, regardless of what some people think. Many people do not believe that there will be a period of time known as the Millennial Reign. They believe that when Jesus returns to the earth, He will then take the Christians to heaven and send the sinners to the lake of fire and that will be the end of it. However, that is not true. Below are a few scriptures that tell us that there **will be** a Millennial Kingdom.

"In the time of those kings, the God of heaven will set up a kingdom that will never be destroyed, nor will it be left to another people. It will crush all those kingdoms and bring them to an end, but it will itself endure forever. This is the meaning of the vision of the rock cut out of a mountain, but not by human hands—a rock that broke the iron, the bronze, the clay, the silver and the gold to pieces..." (Dan. 2:44-45 NIV)

"In my vision at night I looked, and there before me was one like a son of man, coming with the clouds of heaven. He approached the Ancient of Days and was led into his presence. He was given authority, glory and sovereign power; all peoples, nations and men of every language worshiped him. His dominion is an everlasting dominion that will not pass away, and his kingdom is one that will never be destroyed." (Dan. 7:13-14 NIV)

"And the Lord shall be king over all the earth; in that day shall there be one Lord, and his name one." (Zech. 14:9)

"The seventh angel sounded his trumpet, and there were loud voices in heaven, which said: 'The kingdom of the world has become the kingdom of our Lord and of his Christ, and he will reign for ever and ever.'" (Rev. 11:15 NIV)

B. Only The Saints Of God Enter The Millennial Kingdom

"But the saints of the Most High will receive the kingdom and will possess it forever—yes, for ever and ever....until the Ancient of Days came and pronounced judgment in favor of the saints of the Most High, and the time came when they possessed the kingdom....Then the sovereignty, power and greatness of the kingdoms under the whole heaven will be handed over to the saints, the people of the Most High. His kingdom will be an everlasting kingdom, and all rulers will worship and obey him." (Dan. 7: 18, 22, 27 NIV)

Not just any person will enter into the Millennial Kingdom. The requirement to enter into the one thousand years of peace on earth will be that every person that enters **must** be redeemed. Only the saints of God will reign with Christ in His kingdom. As stated earlier, the saints of God include all saints from the beginning of time to the end of the Tribulation period. However, there **will be** those who are yet alive and in the earthly body when the Millennial period begins. But it will be only those who have surrendered their hearts to God that will be able to enter into this period of time with the Lord. It will be only these saved individuals that will live with Christ for one thousand years. No sin and no sinner will be allowed to enter into this Millennial Kingdom.

At the time that Jesus comes to the earth, which is at the close of the Tribulation period, He will destroy all of Satan's activities. As has been shown earlier, Antichrist and the false prophet will be cast alive into the lake of fire and they will remain there for all eternity. Furthermore, all of the armies of the world that are gathered together for the battle of Armageddon will be totally destroyed by Him, and we are told that *"all the fowls were filled with their flesh."* (Rev. 19:21) Satan will be cast into the *"bottomless pit"* and imprisoned there for one thousand years. Thus, all sin and the instigator of sin will no longer be present on the earth. The only people remaining on the earth will be the 144,000 who were sealed by the angels with the seal of God (Rev. 7:1-8) and those who became followers of Christ during the Tribulation period, who have not worshiped the *"beast"* or his image and have not received the mark of Antichrist. Also, there will be others who have not surrendered to God, but yet have not worshiped the *"beast"* nor taken his mark in other nations throughout the earth. (This will be discussed a little later.) Therefore, only those who decide to follow the Lord are allowed to enter into the Millennial Kingdom.

C. The Judgments Of The Nations

As stated above, only those who are redeemed from sin will be allowed to enter into the Millennial Kingdom. Those who have not yet made a decision to surrender to God will be given the chance to make that decision once and for all before the beginning of the *"one thousand years."* How will this be done? God will judge the nations of the earth and each person in every nation **must** decide to either surrender to God's love and peace, or suffer His righteous wrath. As earlier stated, no sin and no sinner will enter into the Millennial period.

1. Judgment Of Israel

"As I live, saith the Lord God, surely with a mighty hand, and with an outstretched arm, and with fury poured out, will I rule over you; And I will bring you out from the peoples, and will gather you out of the countries in which ye are scattered, with a mighty hand, and an outstretched arm, and with fury poured out. And I will bring you into the wilderness of the peoples, and there will I enter into judgment with you face to face. As I entered into judgment with your fathers in the wilderness of the land of Egypt, so will I enter into judgment with you, saith the Lord God. And I will cause you to pass

under the rod, and I will bring you into the bond of the covenant. And I will purge out from among you the rebels, and them that transgress against me; I will bring them forth out of the country where they sojourn, and they shall not enter into the land of Israel; and ye shall know that I am the Lord." (Ezek. 20:33-38)

Some people may think that this scripture is referring to the people of Israel returning to their country from among the many nations and establishing Israel as a nation again as in 1948. However, the scripture above is not referencing that particular event. This is a future event that will take place after the Tribulation period has come to a close.

In Revelation, the last three and one half years of the Tribulation period is said to be 1260 days in length. (Rev. 11:3; 12:6) In other places we are told this period of time will last for *"a time and times and the dividing of time."* (Dan. 7: 25; 12: 7; Rev. 12: 14) We are also told that this period of time is referred to as *"forty and two months."* (Rev. 11: 2; 13: 5) The last half of the Tribulation period is known as the Great Tribulation and it lasts for three and one half years, or 1260 days, or forty-two months. The Tribulation period ends when Antichrist and the false prophet are cast into the lake of fire (Rev. 19: 20) and Satan is bound and cast into the *"bottomless pit"* for a period of *"one thousand years."* (Rev. 20:1-3) However, in Daniel 12:11-12 (NIV) we are told, *"From the time that the daily sacrifice is abolished and the abomination that causes desolation is set up, there will be 1290 days. Blessed is the one who waits for and reaches the end of the 1335 days."* In verse 11 there are 30 days added to the 1260 days. Then in verse 12 we are told that there is an additional 45 days, making a total of 1335 days. This is a total of 75 days added to the end of the 1260 days, which marks the end of the Tribulation period. The Bible does not explain this additional 75-day period. However, it is my belief that a number of things will have to happen that will take some additional time, which I believe that God has allotted for here. The first thing that will have to happen is that the *"fowls"* of the earth will have to have a certain amount of time to consume the flesh of the fallen armies at Armageddon. (Rev. 19:21) Furthermore, the judgment of Israel will take a certain amount of time, as well as the judgment of the Gentile nations. I submit that it could possibly take this extra 75-day period of time for all this to take place **before** the Millennial period begins. Although this is only a speculation, it is very possible.

In Ezekial 20:33-38 we have the account of the people of Israel being brought out of every nation on the earth and brought to *"the wilderness of the peoples."* We are not told where this *"wilderness"* will be. However, because it is the Word of God, we **must** believe that there will be a place which God has set aside in which to bring His people from all parts of the earth. The purpose of the people of Israel being brought to this *"wilderness"* is for judgment. God says that He will *"enter into judgment"* with the people of Israel *"face to face."* The King James Version says that God will *"plead with you face to face. As I pleaded with your fathers in the wilderness of the land of Egypt, so will I plead with you, saith the Lord."* God wants His chosen people to acknowledge Him and accept His son, Jesus, as the Son of God and Israel's Messiah. He wants this to happen so much that He will *"plead"* with them *"face to face."* Those that will except Jesus as Messiah and repent and turn to God will *"pass under the rod"* and God will bring them *"into the bond of the covenant."* This *"rod"* is likened unto a shepherd's staff, which was used for counting the sheep. Possibly the Lord will count those that will enter into *"covenant"* with Him. Those that do not repent, God will *"purge out from among you the rebels, and them that transgress against me. I will bring them forth out of the country where they sojourn, and they shall not enter into the land of Israel."* In other words, those that do not repent and surrender to God will be judged with God's righteous wrath. They will be destroyed as were the rest of the wicked people of the earth. No sin will enter into the Millennial kingdom, and no sin will enter the kingdom of God.

2. The Judgment Of The Gentile Nations

"When the Son of Man comes in his glory, and all the angels with him, he will sit on his throne in heavenly glory. All the nations will be gathered before him, and he will separate the people one from another as a shepherd separates the sheep from the goats. He will put the sheep on his right and the goats on his left. Then the King will say to those on his right, 'Come, you who are blessed by my Father; take your inheritance, the kingdom prepared for you since the creation of the world. For I was hungry and you gave me something to eat, I was thirsty and you gave me something to drink, I was a stranger and you invited me in, I needed clothes and you clothed me, I was sick and you looked after me, I was in prison and you came to visit me.' Then the righteous will answer him, 'Lord, when did we see you hungry and feed you, or thirsty and give you something to drink? When did we see you a stranger and invite you in, or needing clothes and clothe you? When did we see you sick or in prison and go visit you?' The King will reply, 'I tell you the truth. Whatever you did for one of the least of these brothers of mine, you did for me.' Then he will say to those on his left, 'Depart from me, you who are cursed, into eternal fire prepared for the devil and his angels. For I was hungry and you gave me nothing to eat, I was thirsty and you gave me nothing to drink, I was a stranger and you did not invite me in, I needed clothes and you did not clothe me, I was sick and in prison and you did not look after me.' They also will answer, 'Lord, when did we see you hungry or thirsty or a stranger or needing clothes or sick or in prison, and did not help you?' He will reply, 'I tell you the truth, whatever you did not do for one of the least of these, you did not do it for me.' Then they will go away to eternal punishment, but the righteous to eternal life." (St. Matt. 25:31-46 NIV)

After God judges the nation of Israel, His chosen people, He will bring all the remaining nations of the earth together for the purpose of judging them. In the above verses we are told that when Jesus *"comes in his glory, and all the angels with him, he will sit on his throne in heavenly glory."* Jesus will receive His kingdom on the earth and He will sit upon His throne in *"heavenly glory!"* This scene of Jesus sitting on His throne in glory is alone enough to make every saint of God want to shout! This tells us that we will win the victory over Satan!

We are told that the nations of all the earth will be *"gathered before him, and he will separate the people one from another as a shepherd separates the sheep from the goats. He will put the sheep on his right and the goats on his left."* Those on His right are the righteous. They are the people who have not worshiped the *"beast"* and have not received the mark of Antichrist.

These have miraculously survived the horrors of the evil that Antichrist and the false prophet have imposed upon the people during the Tribulation period. These people are the followers of Christ and they have waited patiently for the return of Jesus to the earth to vindicate them from the evil around them. In verses 34-40 we are told that these people did what was right and expected of those who serve the Lord. For their faith and activity in doing the Lord's work, they are rewarded and they will enter *"eternal life."* They will enter into the *"kingdom prepared for you since the creation of the world."*

The *"kingdom prepared for you since the creation of the world"* is what all saints of God will inherit. This *"kingdom prepared...since the creation of the world"* was what God had originally intended for man to live in forever. However, man messed it all up when he committed sin in the Garden of Eden and disobeyed God. God never wanted man to sin and He did not want the world to go the way it did. But because man disobeyed God and basically gave the world to Satan, God had to come up with a plan to regain control of the world and bring it back to what it was originally intended to be.

As stated earlier, the saints of all ages, those who served God while on the earth, then who have died a physical death, will *"reign"* with Christ during the Millennial period. Those people who are yet alive and remain upon the earth after the judgments of Israel and of the Gentile nations will receive their *"inheritance, the kingdom prepared for you since the creation of the world."* The one thousand years of the Millennial period, with Jesus as *"KING OF KINGS, AND LORD OF LORDS,"* and the saints of all ages reigning with Him **IS** the *"inheritance"* of these who will live on the earth in the flesh and blood (earthly) body. These people will live for another *"one thousand years"* and they will continue to *"increase in number"* throughout this period. (Jer. 23:3) These will be both the saved Jews and Gentiles that will enter into the Millennial kingdom after the judgments of Israel and the Gentile nations.

Those that are considered the *"goats"* are put on the Lord's left. In verses 41-45 we are told that these people did not do the things required to be able to enter into the Millennial kingdom. However, in verse 44 they ask, *"Lord, when did we see you hungry or thirsty or a stranger or needing clothes or sick or in prison, and did not help you?"* In the world today, many people throughout the entire world come to the aid of those who are in need. Many nations have come to the aid of earthquake and tsunami victims. But did they do it with love and compassion, or did they do it because they wanted to show others that they did give, thereby making a name for themselves? What is the reasoning in their hearts? They know and God knows their true heart-felt reasons for helping others. Many will ask the Lord this question at the time of judgment. Many will be told *"Depart from me, you who are cursed."* The people that are not repentant and who rebel against God will be turned away and they will *"go away to eternal punishment."* One might say that this seems to be too harsh and that surely God would be more compassionate. Surely God would not turn anyone away. God will have no choice but to turn away those who refuse to obey and repent. He will not allow anyone who is not repentant into the kingdom that was *"prepared...since the creation of the world."* It is not God turning them away; rather, it is they who turn away by their refusal to repent.

It is the belief of this writer that the judgment of both Israel and the Gentile nations will take some period of time to conclude. As stated earlier, it is very probable that the additional 75 days of the prophecy in Daniel 12:11-12 could be to allow for these judgments. When these judgments are completed, the Millennial period will begin. It will last for a period of *"one thousand years."* Some people living on the earth during this time will eventually live to be over 1000 years of age!

D. The Millennial Kingdom Blessed

Possibly another reason for the additional 75 days found in Daniel 12:11-12, will be for God to bless the Millennial kingdom. As stated earlier, this additional 75 day period is not really explained in the Bible. However, it is very probable that this 75-day period of time could be allotted for the purpose of allowing the *"fowls"* of the earth to consume the flesh of the fallen armies of the nations gathered at Armageddon. Furthermore, this period of time could very possibly be allotted for the time it will take for the judgments of both Israel and the Gentile nations. In addition to all of this, God will take the time to bless the Millennial kingdom. It is very possible that this blessing will take place during this 75-day period.

1. The Blessing Of Israel

"I do not want you to be ignorant of this mystery, brothers, so that you may not be conceited: Israel has experienced a hardening in part until the full number of the Gentiles has come in. And so all Israel will be saved, as it is written: 'The deliverer will come from Zion; he will turn godlessness away from Jacob. And this is my covenant with them when I take away their sins.'" (Rom.11:25-27 NIV)

"I will bring back my exiled people Israel; they will rebuild the ruined cities and live in them. They will plant vineyards and drink their wine; they will make gardens and eat their fruit. I will plant Israel in their own land, never again to be uprooted from the land I have given them, says the Lord your God." (Amos 9:14-15 NIV)

For more reading of the blessing of Israel, see Isa. 43:1-7; Jer. 24:6-7; Ezek. 28:25-26; Zeph. 3:20; and Jer. 23:3-8.

2. The Blessing Of The Gentile Nations

"In the last days the mountain of the Lord's temple will be established as chief among the mountains; it will be raised above the hills, and all nations will stream to it. Many peoples will come and say, 'Come, let us go up to the mountain of the Lord, to the house of the God of Jacob. He will teach us his ways, so that we may walk in his paths.' The law will go out from Zion, the word of the Lord from Jerusalem. He will judge between the nations and will settle disputes for many peoples. They will beat their swords into plowshares and their spears into pruning hooks. Nation will not take up sword against nation, nor will they train for war anymore." (Isa. 2:2-4 NIV)

"In that day there will be a highway from Egypt to Assyria. The Assyrians will go to Egypt and the Egyptians to Assyria. The Egyptians and Assyrians will worship together. In that day Israel will be the third, along with Egypt and Assyria, a blessing on the earth. The Lord Almighty will bless them, saying, 'Blessed be Egypt my people, Assyria my handiwork, and Israel my inheritance.'" (Isa. 19:23-25 NIV)

E. What Life Will Be Like During The Millennium

What will life be like on earth during the Millennium? We cannot imagine that people throughout the entire earth will live in peace. With all that has gone on in the earth for thousands of years, can it be possible for man to live in total peace? According to the Word of God, it will be so! The instruments of war will be turned into implements to use in plowing and harvesting crops. Man will not study to make war or plan to take over other countries and peoples. Mankind will have only one King, Who is Jesus. There will be no crime, no sickness, no pain or suffering. Life on earth will be a life of total peace and love. People and the animals in all the earth will be different than they are in this world today.

1. The Animal Kingdom Changed

"The wolf will live with the lamb, the leopard will lie down with the goat, the calf and the lion and the yearling together; and a little child will lead them. The cow will feed with the bear, their young will lie down together, and the lion will eat straw like the ox. The infant will play near the hole of the cobra, and the young child put his hand into the viper's nest. They will neither harm nor destroy on all my holy mountain, for the earth will be full of the knowledge of the Lord as the waters cover the sea." (Isa. 11:6-9 NIV)

In these verses we see that the once ferocious animals are now tame and no longer desire to harm or kill. During the Millennial period, no animal will kill or be killed. The infant can play near the *"hole of the cobra"* and have no fear of harm. A *"young child"* can put his hand in a *"viper's nest"* and not be harmed in any way. We are told that *"they will neither harm nor destroy on all my holy mountain, for the earth will be full of the knowledge of the Lord as the waters cover the sea."* The earth will be God's *"holy mountain."* The animal kingdom will obey the command of God that there will be no harm inflicted on any other animal or human. All the animals on the earth will be completely changed. They will be as they were in the day of Adam and Eve. When mankind committed sin, it was **then** that the animal kingdom became ferocious and vicious, killing and being killed. But in the Millennial kingdom, the animal kingdom will return to what they were before the fall of man.

2. Afflictions And Disease Will Be Gone Forever

"Then will the eyes of the blind be opened and the ears of the deaf unstopped. Then will the lame leap like a deer, and the mute tongue shout for joy. Water will gush forth in the wilderness and streams in the desert." (Isa. 35:5-6 NIV)

"He will wipe away every tear from their eyes. There will be no more death or mourning or crying or pain, for the old order of things has passed away." (Rev. 21:4 NIV)

Life for mankind on earth during the Millennial period will be changed from what it once was. There will be no more sickness or disease. No blind or deaf and no more *"mute tongue."* People throughout the entire earth will not experience pain or death. Never again will anyone mourn for a loved one who has passed on for there will never be any death during this time. The Millennial period will be literally a taste of heaven on earth!

Revelation 21:4 is believed to be a verse referring only to life for those who will live in the New Heaven and New Earth after it is created. However, the Millennial period is literally a foretaste of that coming time. Those that enter into the Millennial period will have a glimpse of what eternity with Christ will truly be like!

There will, at the close of the Millennial period, be a short time of despair. This will be when Satan is to be *"loosed out of his prison"* for *"a little season."* (Rev. 20:3, 7) When Satan is loosed out of his prison, he will go into all the earth and *"deceive the nations which are in the four quarters of the earth."* (Rev. 20:8) (This event will be discussed in the next chapter.) But until Satan is loosed from his prison, life on earth will continue throughout the 1000 years with no pain, death, crying or mourning! There will be no more sickness or afflictions during this great period of time!

3. Jesus To Be *'KING OF KINGS, AND LORD OF LORDS"*

"In that day the Root of Jesse will stand as a banner for the peoples; the nations will rally to him, and his place of rest will be glorious." (Isa. 11:10 NIV)

"The Lord will be king over the whole earth. On that day there will be one Lord, and his name the only name." (Zech. 14:9 NIV)

"He shall be great, and shall be called the Son of the Highest; and the Lord God shall give unto him the throne of his father, David." (St. Lk. 1:32)

"Who being in the very nature God, did not consider equality with God something to be grasped, but made himself nothing, taking the very nature of a servant, being made in human likeness. And being found in appearance as a man, he humbled himself and became obedient to death—even death on a cross! Therefore God exalted him to the highest place and gave him the name that is above every name, that at the name of Jesus every knee should bow, in heaven and on earth and under the earth, and every tongue confess that Jesus Christ is Lord, to the glory of God the Father." (Phil. 2:6-11 NIV)

"…The kingdom of the world has become the kingdom of our Lord and of his Christ, and he will reign for ever and ever." (Rev. 11:15b NIV)

"And he hath on his vesture and on his thigh a name written, KING OF KINGS, AND LORD OF LORDS." (Rev. 19:16)

4. Worship During The Millennial Period

"Then the survivors from all the nations that have attacked Jerusalem will go up year after year to worship the King, the Lord Almighty, and to celebrate the Feast of Tabernacles. If any of the peoples of the earth do not go up to Jerusalem to worship the King, the Lord Almighty, they will have no rain. If the Egyptian people do not go up and take part, they will have no rain. The Lord will bring on them the plague he inflicts on the nations that do not go up to celebrate the Feast of Tabernacles. This will be the punishment of all the nations that do not go up to celebrate the Feast of Tabernacles." (Zech. 14:16-19 NIV)

From all of the scripture that we have seen thus far, we can be assured that there will be people from every nation throughout the world that will enter into the Millennial period. After the judgments of both Israel and the Gentile nations, we are told that the *"survivors from all the nations that have attacked Jerusalem will go up year after year to worship the King, the Lord Almighty, and to celebrate the Feast of Tabernacles."* Therefore, every nation and all peoples will be required to actually go to Jerusalem each year to worship God and to *"celebrate the Feast of Tabernacles."* We must remember that all these people throughout the earth, in every nation, are without sin. They have met the requirement to enter into the Millennial period, which is to repent and accept Jesus as the Son of God and be obedient to God. But as time will go on throughout this 1000 year period, there will be those who will become born into this great time of peace and they will be "conformed" to do what they are taught to do. They will not know sin and they will do only as others teach them. Therefore, the peoples of every nation on the earth will be required to go to Jerusalem every year to worship God and celebrate the Feast of Tabernacles.

There will be those, however, who will evidently not go to Jerusalem to worship God. Because they do not go for this annual event, which is because of disobedience, we are told that God will inflict upon them *"the plague he inflicts on the nations that do not go up to celebrate the Feast of Tabernacles."* He will not send rain on their country, which perhaps they can not afford. The rain keeps the nations free from drought and allows the plants to grow abundantly. The *"plague"* spoken of here is not described in detail other than that it is a plague that God "inflicts on the nations that do not go up to celebrate the Feast of Tabernacles." This plague may be the withholding of rain perhaps for the entire year. Whatever the plague will be, it will not cause death, in that, we are told that there will be no death during this period of time. (Rev. 21:4) This *"punishment,"* although severe, will not bring about disease or death, but will be felt by the people and they will realize why they are being punished. This punishment is not because of sin, because in the Millennial period, sin will not exist. Those born into this period of time may very well disobey God from time to time and they may not go to Jerusalem for the Feast of Tabernacles. Therefore, God will punish them and this will perhaps cause them to go up to Jerusalem the next year to worship and celebrate the Feast of Tabernacles.

5. Population Increases During The Millennial Period

"This is what the Sovereign Lord says: When I gather the people of Israel from the nations where they have been scattered, I will show myself holy among them in the sight of the nations. They will live in their own land, which I gave to my servant Jacob. They will live there in safety and will build houses and plant vineyards; they will live in

safety when I inflict punishment on all their neighbors who maligned them. Then they will know that I am the Lord their God." (Ezek. 28:25-26 NIV)

"And I will bring again the captivity of my people of Israel, and they shall build the waste cities, and inhabit them; and they shall plant vineyards, and drink their wine; they shall also make gardens, and eat the fruit of them. And I will plant them upon their land, and they shall no more be pulled up out of their land which I have given them, saith the Lord, thy God." (Amos 9:14-15)

"I myself will gather the remnant of my flock out of all the countries where I have driven them and will bring them back to their pasture, where they will be fruitful and increase in number." (Jer. 23:3 NIV)

These verses of scripture indicate that the population of the people living in the earth during the Millennial period will increase. It is a fact that there will be people who will live on the earth in every nation, and that they will rebuild the ruined cities and live in homes. They will *"plant vineyards"* and they will plant *"gardens"* and people will be nourished by these means. It is my belief that not only will these who enter the Millennial period live throughout the entire 1000 years, but they will also *"increase in number."* Therefore, because we are told that the inhabitants of the earth will *"increase in number,"* children will be born to people during this time. Jeremiah 23:3 plainly states that the people will *"increase in number."* I do not see any other way around this fact. Also, in Isaiah 11: 6 and 8 we are told the *"a little child shall lead them"* and *"the nursing child shall play on the hole of the asp."* Therefore, this is proof that there will be people living during the 1000 years of the Millennium, and they will have children and these will grow up and have children and this cycle will continue until the 1000 years are finished.

At the close of the Millennial period, there will be multiple thousands of people living on the earth. This will be when Satan will be *"loosed from his prison"* for a short time. In the next chapter, the Final Revolt that Satan leads against God will be discussed. Satan will successfully deceive many of these who were born into the Millennial kingdom and cause many to turn from God.

Chapter Nine
THE CONSUMMATION—THE FINAL RE-VOLT

At the close of the Millennial period, several events will take place. I call this the consummation because of the fact that from the close of the Millennial period, God will bring everything to a close, or to a completion. Immediately at the end of the *"one thousand years"* of Christ's reign on the earth, Satan will be *"loosed a little season."* Once released *"out of his prison,"* Satan will resume his diabolical scheme of trying to overthrow God and His kingdom. He will begin to deceive the people in all the nations of the earth and sway them to follow him into battle against Jesus and the Holy City of God, Jerusalem.

Satan Loosed From The Bottomless Pit

"...after that he must be loosed a little season." (Rev. 20:3)

"And when the thousand years are ended, Satan shall be loosed out of his prison,..." (Rev. 20:7)

In the seventh chapter of this book it was discovered that Satan would be bound and imprisoned in the *"bottomless pit,"* or abyss, for a period of *"one thousand years."* During this one thousand-year period the people that live on the earth will live a peaceful life without sin. They will *"increase in number"* (Jer. 23:3) during this period of time and the population of the earth will most likely become a tremendous number. However, the people that are born into this period of time are basically "conformed" to live peacefully and they are taught to worship God. They go up to Jerusalem year after year to worship God and to celebrate the Feast of Tabernacles. (Zech. 14:16-19) But these people born into this Millennial kingdom are only "conformed" to live this way, for they are taught this way of life from birth. They know nothing of sin and are not tempted to commit sin, for the "tempter," who is Satan, is bound and in prison in the *"bottomless pit"* and is not free to cause temptation to enter the minds and lives of these people.

At the close of the Millennial period, however, Satan is to be set free from his prison *"for a little season."* The NIV says that Satan *"must be set free for a short time."* His freedom will be short lived. He will undoubtedly be filled with ferocious anger and he will come out of the *"bottomless pit"* with the single purpose of trying to destroy God and His Kingdom.

A. Millions Deceived By Satan

"And when the thousand years are ended, Satan shall be loosed out of his prison, And shall go to deceive the nations which are in the four quarters of the earth, Gog and Magog, to gather them together to battle; the number of whom is as the sand of the sea." (Rev. 20: 7-8)

These verses alone, in my opinion, proves that there are literally millions of people to be born into the Millennial kingdom. If people are not to live on the earth for this one thousand-year period of time, and if they do not *"increase in number"* during this time, then who would Satan be able to deceive? There would be no person on the earth for him **to** deceive! Satan cannot deceive those who are already dead and resurrected. Therefore, there must be a large group of people in every nation of the earth for him to deceive. We are told that Satan will *"deceive the nations which are in the four quarters of the earth, Gog and Magog, to gather them together to battle; the number of whom is as the sand of the sea."* Gog and Magog were first heard of in Ezekiel and are the names referencing the countries to the north of Israel. But here, they refer to the names of all the nations that are to be deceived by Satan. Satan deceives these nations and causes them to come together to do battle and we are told the *"number of whom are as the sand of the sea."* Can you imagine the countless number this will be? No one can count the number of the sand of the sea! This is in reference to a great multitude of people who will be deceived.

How can Satan deceive this large number of people? It is believed that because the people that are born into the Millennial kingdom have not had the opportunity to choose between righteousness and unrighteousness, this time of Satan's luring will give them this opportunity to choose God or Satan. From what we see in this verse, a great multitude will choose to follow Satan rather than follow God.

B. The Final Battle Or Revolt

"They marched across the breadth of the earth and surrounded the camp of God's people, the city he loves." (Rev. 20:9a NIV)

Satan deceives the nations of the earth and causes them to prepare for battle and brings them *"across the breadth of the earth and surrounded the camp of God's people, the city he loves."* Satan hates God and His people so much that he foolishly tries to do battle against them. The *"city"* that God loves is none other than Jerusalem. Therefore, it is around Jerusalem where this final revolt is to take place. For whatever reason Satan gives, he convinces the people that he deceives to come against God and His people.

C. Satan And His Followers Destroyed

"...But fire came down from heaven and devoured them. And the Devil, who deceived them, was thrown into the lake of burning sulfur, where the beast and the false prophet had been thrown. They will be tormented day and night for ever and ever." (Rev. 20:9b-10 NIV)

When the armies of all the nations gather around Jerusalem to wage a final battle against God and His people, something happens. I do not believe one shot will be fired from anyone, or that even one person will kill another, when they come against God and His people. The intent is there, but they do not get the chance to do anything. We are told that *"fire came down out of heaven and devoured them."* God puts a complete and final end to Satan and his armies here! He destroys the wicked armies of the earth and He casts Satan into the eternal lake of fire *"where the beast and the false prophet had been thrown."* We are told that this lake of fire is where Satan and those who have decided to follow him will spend all eternity. They will suffer the torment of that place *"for ever and ever."*

The final revolt that Satan brings against God and His people proves to bring about Satan's total defeat. During this final revolt, literally millions of people who have been deceived and chose to follow Satan will have been destroyed. Therefore, the only remaining people on the earth will be those that have chosen to remain true to God. Once Satan is destroyed, there will once again be total peace on earth. There will be no sin and no sinners left on the earth at this time.

In preparation for the judgment of all the wicked and the creation of the New Heaven and New Earth, this earth will become purged. In 2 Peter 3: 10-13 we are given the account of the purging of the heavens and the earth. When this purging is done, God will gather all of His people from throughout the entire earth, in much the same manner as He did when the saints of the Church Age was *"caught up."* The current heavens and earth will then be purged. We are told the *"heavens will disappear with a roar; the elements will be destroyed by fire, and the earth and everything in it will be laid bare."* I believe that this purging of the *"heavens and earth"* will coincide with the destruction of Satan and those that are deceived when God sends *"fire"* upon the earth to destroy them when they surround God's Holy city. Once this is done, God will judge those who come before Him. If a person's name is not found in the *"Book of Life,"* he will be cast into the lake of fire for all eternity.

Chapter Ten
THE CONSUMMATION—THE GREAT WHITE THRONE JUDGMENT

"Then I saw a great white throne and the One Who was seated upon it, from Whose presence and from the sight of Whose face earth and sky fled away and no place was found for them. I also saw the dead, great and small; they stood before the throne, and books were opened. Then another book was opened, which is the Book of Life. And the dead were judged (sentenced) by what they had done (their whole way of feeling and acting, their aims and endeavors) in accordance with what was recorded in the books. And the sea delivered up the dead who were in it, Death and Hades (the state of death or disembodied existence) surrendered the dead in them; and all were tried and their cases determined by what they had done— according to their motives, aims and works. Then death and Hades (the state of death or disembodied existence) were thrown into the lake of fire. This is the second death, the lake of fire. And if any one's (name) was not found recorded in the Book of Life, he was hurled into the lake of fire." (Rev. 20:11-15 Amp. Bible)

The author, John, sees a *"great white throne and the One Who was seated upon it."* This is God Himself seated upon this throne. He is here for the purpose of judging. The Amplified Version says that He is there to sentence those who come before Him. We are told that the One sitting upon the throne is the One *"from Whose presence and from Whose face earth and sky fled away and no place was found for them."* As stated earlier, the earth and the heavens will be destroyed. At the time of the final revolt, led by Satan, God then will cause this present earth to become purged. The *"heavens will disappear with a roar; the elements will be destroyed by fire."* We are told that *"the earth and everything in it will be laid bare."* (2 Pet. 3:10 NIV) The Amplified Bible says *"the heavens will vanish (pass away) with a thunderous crash, and the (material) elements (of the universe) will be dissolved with fire, and the earth and the works that are upon it will be burned up."* Therefore, it is the opinion of this writer that the heavens and the earth as we know it today will be totally destroyed and will not be found. The people who will be living on the earth at the time of this event will be translated, or *"caught up,"* to be with the Lord. When the event of the great white throne judgment is complete, God will create a new heaven and new earth for all to live on and enjoy for all eternity.

We are told that the wicked dead, *"great and small; they stood before the throne and the books were opened."* All of the wicked dead, no matter who they were in life on earth, will be here before this throne. They will one by one come before the Judge, Who is God Almighty, and answer for their deeds while upon the earth. Not one person will escape this judgment! We are told that these will be sentenced *"by what they had done (their whole way of feeling and acting, their aims and endeavors) in accordance with what was recorded in the books."* These books are records of all the things every sinner did while alive on the earth. Every deed and every secret will be revealed. Nothing will escape the eyes of God and He will judge according to what is written in these books.

After the wicked people have been sentenced, we are told that they will be *"thrown into the lake of fire."* They have died a physical death and spiritual death, which was the completion of the first death. But now they are going to experience the *"second death,"* which is the lake of fire. We are told that *"if any one's (name) was not found in the Book of Life, he was hurled into the lake of fire."* As has been stated many times throughout this book, no sin and no sinner will be able to enter the Kingdom of God.

This event is also the final resurrection. The second resurrection of the dead is that of the resurrection of the wicked from the beginning of time. The first resurrection is that of all the saints of God. All wicked souls that lived upon the earth from the beginning of time will be resurrected here and these will go before God for judgment. As stated above, they will all be judged for their deeds that they had done while living upon the earth. They will answer to God for their actions and for their secret deeds that they think no one will ever know. Then they will be cast into the *"second death,"* which is the *"lake of fire,"* where they will be tormented forever and ever.

Chapter Eleven

THE CONSUMMATION—THE NEW HEAVEN AND NEW EARTH

"Then I saw a new sky (heaven) and a new earth; for the former sky and the former earth had passed away (vanished), and there no longer existed any sea. And I saw the holy city, the new Jerusalem, descending out of heaven from God, all arrayed like a bride beautified and adorned for her husband. Then I heard a mighty voice from the throne and I perceived its distinct words, saying, See! The Abode of God is with men, and He will live (encamp, tent) among them, and they shall be His people and God shall personally be with them and be their God." (Rev. 21:1-3 Amp. Bible)

John now sees a *"new sky (heaven) and a new earth; for the former sky and the former earth had passed away (vanished), and there no longer existed any sea."* As was stated earlier, the earth and the heavens that we currently have today will someday be destroyed. God said, *"For, behold, I create new heavens and a new earth, and the former shall not be remembered, nor come into mind."* (Isa. 65:17) After the final revolt against God's people and His Holy City, the armies of the nations, led by Satan, will be destroyed by fire that comes down from God out of heaven. At this time the heavens and the earth will then be destroyed. (2 Pet. 3:10) It will be at this time when all the wicked from beginning of time will be resurrected and brought before God for judgment. Those who did not rebel against God and who were still alive on the earth will have been translated, or caught up in much the same manner as were the saints of the Church Age, and they will have been changed from earthly bodies to that of glorified bodies. But the heavens and the earth will be destroyed and will no longer be found. *"For as the new heavens and the new earth, which I shall make, shall remain before me, saith the Lord, so shall your seed and your name remain."* (Isa. 66:22) Suddenly there will be a new heaven and a new earth created. We are told that this new earth will not have any sea. (Rev.21:1) It would seem that the entire new earth will be covered by land with the exception of the *"pure river of water of life."* (Rev. 22:1) It will be on this new earth where saints of all ages will remain for all eternity.

John then sees *"the holy city, the new Jerusalem, descending out of heaven from God, all arrayed like a bride beautified and adorned for her husband."* In the next verse, we are told that this is the *"abode of God"* which is now to be *"with men, and He will live (encamp, tent) among them, and they shall be His people and God shall personally be with them and be their God."* For all eternity, God will dwell among people in the new earth. Forever will those that have lived for the Lord on the old earth be in the presence of Almighty God! *"My tabernacle also shall be with them; yea, I will be their God, and they shall be my people."* (Ezek. 37:27)

A. All Things Made New

"God will wipe away every tear from their eyes, and death shall be no more, neither shall there be anguish—sorrow and mourning—nor grief nor pain any more; for the old conditions and the former order of things have passed away. And He Who is seated on the throne said, See! I make all things new. Also He said, Record this, for these sayings are faithful—accurate, incorruptible and trustworthy—and true (genuine)." (Rev. 21:4-5 Amp. Bible)

During the time of the Millennial period, people will have gotten a taste of what it will be like when God will create the new heaven and new earth. During that period, they, too, were free of pain and death. They did not suffer anguish, disease or sickness. It will be the same in the new earth. God will *"wipe away every tear from their eyes, and death shall be no more, neither shall there be anguish—sorrow and mourning—nor grief nor pain any more."* God will have made all things new, for *"the old conditions and the former order of things have passed away."* We are told that God *"will swallow up death in victory; and the Lord God will wipe away tears from all faces; and the rebuke of his people shall he take away from all the earth; for the Lord hath spoken it."* (Isa. 25:8) Those that will be with the Lord in the new heaven and new earth will forever enjoy the tenderness and love of God, our Father! We are further told that *"the ransomed of the Lord shall return, and come to Zion with songs and everlasting joy upon their heads; they shall obtain joy and gladness, and sorrow and sighing shall flee away."* (Isa. 35:10)

God tells us, *"See! I make all things new."* God loves His people so much that He will *"do a new thing; now it shall spring forth."* (Isa. 43:19) God wants John to *"Record this, for these sayings are faithful—accurate, incorruptible and trustworthy—and true (genuine)."* This will be the eternal home of those who will serve the Lord and follow His ways. Those who turn away from God have nothing to gain except eternal torment in the lake of fire. Life on this present earth is hard enough, and we suffer so much hurt and pain. It will be really nice to be able to spend all eternity experiencing the joys and peace of God! We see enough hell on this earth today. Why would anyone want to go to a place of torment and suffer that tremendous pain for all eternity? God does not want anyone to go to that place. The lake of fire was prepared for Satan and his evil angels, not for man. (St. Matt. 25:41) But man has to choose the course he will take. Sadly, many will make the wrong choice.

B. The Inheritance

"And He (further) said unto me, It is done! I am the Alpha and the Omega, the Beginning and the End. To the thirsty I (Myself) will give water without price from the fountain (springs) of the water of Life. He who is victorious shall inherit all these things, and I will be God to him and he shall be My son." (Rev. 21:6-7 Amp. Bible)

Here, John says that the one who was speaking to him said, *"It is done! I am the Alpha and the Omega, the Beginning and the End."* Jesus is referred to as the *"Alpha and Omega, the beginning and the ending."* (Rev. 1:8) We are thus given the promise from Jesus *"To the thirsty I (Myself) will give water without price from the fountain (springs) of the water of Life."* Those that are *"victorious shall inherit all these things,"* Jesus says, *"and I will be God to him and he shall be My son."* Jesus and the Father are one. Jesus said, *"So that they all may be one (just) as You, Father, are in Me and I in You,...(even) as We are one."* (St. John 17:21-22 Amp.) Those that endure and become the victorious will inherit the Kingdom of God! Therefore, we will become one with Jesus, and will live with Him throughout all eternity in the Kingdom of God. As Christians we strive to become one with Jesus each day. We must continue to work toward that end. As we do so, we will eventually inherit life eternal in God's presence. Praise the Lord!

C. Doom Of The Wicked

"But as for the cowards and the ignoble and the contemptible and the cravenly lacking in courage and the cowardly submissive; and as for the unbelieving and faithless; and as for the depraved and defiled with abominations; and as for murderers and the lewd and adulterous and the practicers of magic arts and the idolaters (those who give supreme devotion to any one or anything other than God)

and all liars (those who knowingly convey untruth by word or deed, all of these shall have) their part in the lake that blazes with fire and brimstone. This is the second death." (Rev. 21:8 Amp. Bible)

In this single verse we are told that all those who do these things, such as adultery, idolatry, those who practice sexual perversions, those who practice magic arts, and unbelievers, these will not inherit the Kingdom of God. We are told that they will have *"their part in the lake that blazes with fire and brimstone."* No one who has **any** sin in his or her life will ever see the Kingdom of God. They will **never** have a part in it! The only way to assure one's self of entering the joys of the Lord and spending eternity with Christ is to **accept** Him as Savior and **live** for Him each moment of each day. Those who do not believe and do not accept Jesus as Lord of his life will have his place in the lake of fire. They will experience the *"second death."* The *"second death"* is eternal separation from God and eternal torment in the *"lake of fire."* Again I ask, why would anyone want to spend eternity in torment?

D. The New Jerusalem

"One of the seven angels who had the seven bowls full of the seven last plagues came and said to me, 'Come, I will show you the bride, the wife of the Lamb.' And he carried me away in the Spirit to a mountain great and high, and showed me the Holy City, Jerusalem, coming down out of heaven from God. It shone with the glory of God, and its brilliance was like that of a very precious jewel, like a jasper, clear as crystal." (Rev. 21:9-11 NIV)

John says that one of the *"seven angels who had the seven bowls full of the seven last plagues"* came to him and took him to a *"mountain great and high."* There he sees the *"Holy City, Jerusalem"* coming down out of heaven from God. He said it *"shone with the glory of God, and its brilliance was like that of a very precious jewel, like a jasper, clear as crystal."* He says that this *"Holy City, Jerusalem"* is called the *"bride of the Lamb."* It was mentioned earlier in this book that the bride of the Lamb is the Church. One would think that this would be considered to be somewhat contradictory. However, it is not. It is the *"Holy City, Jerusalem"* that is being spoken of here, which cannot be considered a bride or a wife. Rather the *"Holy City, Jerusalem,"* is represented **as** *"the bride of the Lamb,"* in that, it is the home of the saints for eternity, and that it is to be **compared** to a bride. The Holy City, Jerusalem is related to the Lamb in an intimate manner as the home of his bride, the saints.

The city that comes down out of heaven from God is called the *"bride of the Lamb"* possibly in part because the saints of the Church Age now dwell in this city. Also, the guests and friends who were invited to the marriage of the Lamb, the Old Testament and Tribulation saints, will occupy the city. In this manner, the *"Holy City, Jerusalem"* would be called the *"bride of the Lamb"* insomuch as Jesus is intimately related to those within the Holy City.

The remaining verses of scripture in Revelation 21 and Revelation 22:1-5 ascribes to the beauty of the Holy City. We will not live in a city on this earth as beautiful or radiant as this city is! John describes the city from both an outward appearance and an inward appearance. When Jesus said that He was going to *"prepare a place"* (St. John 14:2) for us, He will do a magnificent job! If you want to know what heaven will be like, all you need do is read Revelation 21:9-27 and 22:1-5. The future home of the righteous will be far greater than any place found on this earth! Oh, the joy! Oh, the splendor of that great Holy City! Heaven is a real place, and those that continually put their trust in Jesus will live forever in that marvelous Holy City!

Finally, Jesus says, *"Behold, I come quickly. Blessed is he that keepeth the words of the prophecy of this book."* (Rev. 22:7) Furthermore, He said, *"And, behold, I come quickly, and my reward is with me, to give every man according as his work shall be."* (Rev. 22:12) Jesus **IS** coming soon! I ask that if you are not now ready to meet Him when He comes, will you take the time to ask Jesus into your heart? If you will, He **will** come and He **will** be your Lord and Savior! I pray that you will be found watching and ready for His return.

In closing, I would like to leave you with the following verses of scripture.

"He who testifies to these things says, 'Yes, I am coming soon.' Amen. Come, Lord Jesus. The grace of the Lord Jesus be with God's people. Amen." (Rev. 22:20-21 NIV)

Please remember to keep *"Looking for that blessed hope and the glorious appearing of the great God and our Savior, Jesus Christ."* (Ti. 2:13)

Printed in the United States
52559LVS00002B/544

9 781424 135295